Written with the heart of a mot [...]
Why? is not only profound, but al[...] [...]
is not just *about* suffering; it is written by one who *knows* suffering, for
others who are suffering themselves.
Os Guinness, author of Unspeakable: Facing Up to the Challenge of Evil

Lucid, empathetic and biblical, this engaging treatment of the enigma
of human suffering speaks to both the confused mind and the aching
heart, with wisdom, logic and grace. I warmly commend it.
David J. Jackman, Past President, The Proclamation Trust

I love the way Sharon wrestles with the truth. She turns it inside out
and inspects its seams. She shakes it to see what falls out. She looks at
it through the grid of real life and defines it with doctrinally solid,
scripturally sound conclusions. Both moving and challenging.
Jennifer Kennedy Dean, author of Live a Praying Life, *and Executive
Director of The Praying Life Foundation*

Sharon writes with sensitivity and insight about the painful reality of
suffering in our world which will in one way or another affect us all. I
wholeheartedly recommend this book to anyone asking the deep
questions of life.
Amy Orr-Ewing, UK Director, Oxford Centre for Christian Apologetics

When I was sixteen, my sports career was called into question when I
was run over by a speed boat and got caught in the propellers. Sharon's
book puts words and reason to what I instinctively knew in my heart
the day I became an amputee: God loves me, God is good, God is
all-powerful, and God was mourning the loss of my leg alongside me.
I flipped between anger and thankfulness that my life had been spared,
but the experience of God's peace was constant. Sharon does a brilliant
and honest job of explaining this paradox.
Stefanie Reid, professional athlete and British Paralympic medallist

Sharon Dirckx

Foreword by Ravi Zacharias

why?

Looking at God, evil
& personal suffering

INTER-VARSITY PRESS
Norton Street, Nottingham NG7 3HR, England
Email: ivp@ivpbooks.com
Website: www.ivpbooks.com

First published 2013

British Library Cataloguing in Publication Data
A catalogue record for this book is available from the British Library.

ISBN: 978–1–84474–619–4

Set in Dante 11.5/14pt
Typeset in Great Britain by CRB Associates, Potterhanworth, Lincolnshire
Printed and bound in Great Britain by Ashford Colour Press, Gosport, Hampshire

*Inter-Varsity Press publishes Christian books that are true to the Bible and that
communicate the gospel, develop discipleship and strengthen the church for its mission
in the world.*

*Inter-Varsity Press is closely linked with the Universities and Colleges Christian
Fellowship, a student movement connecting Christian Unions in universities and colleges
throughout Great Britain, and a member movement of the International Fellowship of
Evangelical Students. Website: www.uccf.org.uk*

For my husband Conrad

Contents

Acknowledgments

This book has been the work of more than one person. Thank you to all who have asked the 'why?' questions; I hope this book is of some help on your journey. Thank you to my editor Eleanor Trotter and the team at IVP, for commissioning the book and for this opportunity to write. Thank you, Frances, Will, Grace, Charles and Rachel, for your time and willingness to be real. Your stories have *made* this book. Thanks must go to my mum for patiently transcribing the interviews and saving me hours of work in the process.

Thank you to Caroline Sants for your hospitality during my final stages of writing. I am also very grateful to Kate Blanshard, Simon Wenham and Vince Vitale for commenting on the manuscript so helpfully.

Thank you to all who have prayed faithfully as I have written, especially Vicky and Joyce; my prayer group with Rachel, Lynne, Jenny and Jenny; and all the superb Monday Mums at St Andrew's Church, Oxford. Thank you to the whole team at OCCA and RZIM for your prayers and support, especially Nancy Gifford and Ruth McGarahan.

Special thanks go to my parents, Pauline and Dennis, for your love and sacrifices over many years. In many different ways this book would not have been written without your help!

Extra special thanks must go to my husband Conrad. Thank you for believing in my fledgling idea five years ago and encouraging me to write. Thank you for creating the space needed, for poring over the manuscript, for being so selfless, so patient and so prayerful. Finally, thank you for being willing to share your own story, which has galvanized this book.

Foreword

It has been said, 'Never morning wore to evening but that some heart did break.' The famed preacher Philip Brooks once noted, 'If you preach to a hurting heart, you will never lack for an audience.' Pain, suffering and evil are indisputable realities and present the sharpest edge of criticism against God's existence. In fact, all one needs to do is wake up and read the newspapers and one would wonder where God is in the grand scheme of things. History unfolds before our eyes, and suffering is writ large in the human experience.

One is tempted to ask if God is in control. In that question lie the heart and mind of the problem. What kind of world are we asking for? What shape would things take if we were in control? Certainly, we would wrestle with the idea of a world free from pain and suffering. Until we get there, we keep asking, *Why this kind of world?*

Sharon Dirckx wrestles with these and other difficult questions in her fine book, *Why?* And Sharon is no ordinary questioner: she has a PhD in brain imaging from the University of Cambridge and has held research positions in the USA and the University of Oxford. She is also a member of the first class of graduates at our Oxford Centre for Christian Apologetics and is now an Academic Tutor at OCCA.

But make no mistake; Sharon is not an academic unfamiliar with pain. Indeed, as a wife and mother, she writes out of her own experience of suffering alongside her husband who struggles with a chronic and debilitating illness. Anyone who has walked this road – as I have with my fragile back – understands the stabbing questions and confusion when suffering seems to be all-consuming. As Sharon notes in her book, 'The question, "Why . . . ?" occurs 510 times in the Bible. Its pages are packed with people being extremely real with God about their circumstances, expressing a range of human emotions, from the depths of despair and depression to elation, anger and beyond.' In conversation with her on such matters, one can readily see how clear she is in her thinking, how caring she is as a person and how relevant she is in her answers. This book brings those combined strengths. She invites her readers to consider these questions, and offers refreshing encouragement and insight along the way.

I am pleased to recommend Sharon's work to you and trust you will find it a valuable resource in your search for answers.

Ravi Zacharias, author and speaker

Introduction

We only have to turn on the news for a few seconds to be bombarded with human suffering in all its forms. Natural disasters and famines strike down hundreds of thousands; wars tear apart families; suicide bombers wreak havoc in the Middle East, and now the West as well. Traffic accidents end life in an instant. Stabbings, burglaries, corruption and bribery are daily occurrences. We cannot be blamed for asking, 'Why? Why do these things happen?'

Yet suffering is not just out there in the form of news headlines; it is also very personal. Perhaps you are reading this, knowing all too well the pain of losing a loved one, or the pain of divorce, or the pain of infertility, or the pain of mental illness, or of physical sickness, or the pain of struggling with an eating disorder, or with sexual identity, or the pain of being relentlessly bullied. Suffering is not just something we hear about on the news, but something that is woven into everyday life. In writing a book on suffering, there is certainly no shortage of material.

Our very natural response is to ask the question: 'Why is this happening to me?' 'Why?' is one of the very first questions a child asks, and there seems to be something intrinsically human about asking it. But if you have asked 'Why?', surely this raises an interesting thought: to whom are you addressing the question?

Do you know? Does it matter? Our society tells us that there is a variety of different options out there. In situations of suffering, some would turn to Eastern meditation as a source of strength, some to nature itself, others to the Allah of Islam, others to the God of Judaism or Christianity, and still others would say they are not appealing to anyone or anything, but merely letting off steam into the unknown.

An indicator of whether a belief system is true or not lies in its ability to make sense of the real world. In other words, true beliefs can be lived out practically and offer explanations that help us make sense of life, rather than throwing us into further confusion. So in the case of pain and suffering, are all the religious options equally valid crutches pulled out to get us through the tough times, and then binned once we are back on our feet? Or do some seem to ring true more than others? Where do the most satisfying answers come from?

There are two purposes to this book. The first is to respond to some of the questions people ask about suffering. If God is real, then there must be persuasive reasons as to why evil exists and why suffering (the impact of evil on a person's life) is allowed. I will consider two different types of evil. In chapters 1, 2 and 3 I will deal with moral evil, in other words, evil relating to how people behave. In chapter 7 I will examine natural evil, in other words, evil that originates from nature itself, either in the form of earthquakes and tsunamis, or in the form of disease and sickness. The second purpose of this book is to share with you the stories of normal people who have suffered (and still do) in many different ways, and whose practical experience is that one particular faith does indeed stand out amongst the rest. These people are Christians, and their stories will unwrap their experience of God in their suffering. I interviewed each person, and the words you will read are very much their own. In some cases, names have been changed, but the stories are authentic.

Let me also say what this book is not. It is not attempting to say that Christians have all the answers. Sometimes eager

Christians can stray into arrogance or insensitivity by giving the impression that we know the reason and purpose behind all suffering and every tragic event. As you will see, many of those who have shared their stories are yet to receive answers to the 'why?' of their suffering, and indeed may never do so. Christians do not have all the answers. But does this mean there are no answers at all? When faced with suffering, people often respond with: 'Surely a loving God would not have allowed this to happen!' or 'Does God care about this?' or 'Why doesn't he do something?' In other words, people assume that, given the presence of evil in our world, God either does not exist or else he is weak, malicious or indifferent to our suffering. I would like to show you that, even though we don't understand everything, it is still possible to believe in a God who is completely loving, completely in control of events and intimately concerned with the details of our lives, and yet also acknowledge the reality of evil and suffering. Not only that, but I would like to show you that seeing life from this perspective helps us make more, not less, sense of our hurting world.

Frances's story

We first knew about Millie when we discovered I was pregnant in July 2006. With two straightforward pregnancies behind us and two healthy young boys, we didn't anticipate any problems. At the twenty-week scan the consultant told us, 'There is no easy way to say this: your baby has got holoprosencephaly, a rare and severe brain abnormality.' If our baby survived birth, the chances were that she might live for days or weeks, maybe even months, but definitely not years.

We headed off to the Lake District to join friends, in a bit of a blur and grieving the loss of our healthy baby. We had so many unanswered questions: What exactly was holoprosencephaly? What did this mean for us as a family? As soon as we got back, we began to try to find answers.

We spent some time looking up holoprosencephaly on the internet, and talking to doctors to get an idea of the severity and life expectancy. The consultant seemed to indicate that Millie was somewhere around the middle: not the most severe case but certainly not the least affected. We were anxious that a long life expectancy with a very severe abnormality would require one-to-one care. How would that impact on our two active boys? It seemed that many babies didn't survive a year, but beyond that was much less clear. We decided to have further investigations, and so went up to London to be seen by a world expert team of obstetricians. There were about ten or twelve people in the room, all looking at the ultrasound scan. The two really tough questions that I was trying to get my head around were: would Millie suffer if we went ahead with the pregnancy, and would she know me as her mother? I asked both, and was told that it was likely she would choke to death and that she wouldn't have any knowledge of me as a mother. They offered us a termination that evening, but we just needed time to think things through.

We sat on the coach feeling our lowest yet. Did we have a choice? If what the London experts had said was true, could we inflict that suffering on our child? If life would be unbearable for her, how could we continue with the pregnancy? But medicine is rarely that black and white, and our neonatologist reassured us a few days later that there would be ways in which Millie's distress could be managed. The alternative, a lethal injection *in utero* at twenty-two weeks, did not bear thinking about. But how would we cope? How would we balance the needs of our severely disabled daughter with the needs of our lively young boys? This decision seemed too difficult. Too beyond us. There were so many things to consider.

Both of us have a strong belief in God. Having struggled to know what to do, my husband prayed, 'Lord, we can't do this on our own. Please help us to make this decision.' The next day God spoke clearly to us. Through a chance conversation with a friend of a friend who I knew was a Christian, we were recommended a book about another couple with a distressing diagnosis at twenty weeks who had continued with their pregnancy. I immediately bought the book. On leaving the bookshop, my eyes were drawn to the sign on the door: 'Books Change Lives'. When my husband got home, we read it together that night. The couple's story was very uplifting, celebrating the precious life of their unborn child. God had heard and answered our prayer. We knew what to do and felt at peace about the decision.

Emilia Grace Scott-Brown was born at 9am on 20 February 2007, just two days early, weighing 6 lb 2 oz. She was surprisingly strong when she entered the world. Millie was very much with us, and it was incredibly moving to meet her. She did have an unusual face, with a soft squishy nose and cleft lip, and her eyes were slightly different. But to us she was beautiful Millie and we loved her from that moment.

After the initial few hours it was evident that she would live long enough to need feeding. Bottle and breast feeding were ruled out, and we had to learn how to feed her through a tube into her nose. Millie responded well, and so we transferred to Helen House, the first children's hospice, which amazingly was situated a five-minute walk from our home. The welcome was overwhelming. Millie's room was decorated with her name-plate and a brand new Moses basket. For a week we were cushioned from the outside world and allowed time to be with our precious baby, learning how to look after her while our boys played happily together. Then we were ready to leave Helen House and realize one of our greatest hopes: to bring Millie home.

We tried to lead as normal a life as possible. Millie would come with us on the school run and she soon became quite a feature at school – indeed some of the children and teachers became really fond of her. The local community took her to their hearts and people embraced her differences. Millie spent many happy hours lying on her mat, kicking her legs and reaching out for her sensory toys. She was definitely conscious of the different people around her. She could tell especially when Martin and I were there. She also knew when the house was filled with the noise of her lively brothers. Nurses came to our home twice a week to care for Millie, play with her and read stories to her. Two nights a week Millie's grandpa looked after her, to give us a reasonable night's sleep. Since we could not leave her by herself for fear that she would have a fit or the tube would be dislodged, she spent hours in our arms, responding to the closeness of those who loved her.

But life was also hard for Millie, and it was a constant challenge to try to make things better for her. There were times when she would be constantly sick. Sometimes her tube would come out, and I'd have to put it back in. This was evidently uncomfortable for her, although with practice I became skilled at doing it, and Millie did not notice so much. We had to be able to do it wherever we were, and in the middle of the night if necessary. Millie's brain would not let her settle at night, so she required medicine to help her sleep. Many of my most cherished times with her were spent in the quiet moments, when the boys were in bed and she cuddled into me and slowly drifted off to sleep.

After four or five months Millie developed fits, and we needed a whole new range of medicines to control them. After the first one she went very grey, and my son Thomas, then four, asked me if she was dying. I did not know. We dashed round to Helen House, our lifeline in times of emergency. Soon afterwards the doctor, who had reassured us initially, sat down and put her arm around me. 'You know,' she said, 'there's quite a chance that Millie will die in one of these fits.'

Those months were both hard and enriching. Life's minor stresses became irrelevant, and we learnt to live life to the full, celebrating each milestone. When Millie was six months old we had a big party for her, not knowing whether she would ever reach her first birthday. There were times when the strain was simply unbearable. On one occasion we summoned up the courage to go abroad for a long weekend, leaving Millie in Helen House. She hadn't been in great form before we left, but the doctors thought she was strong enough for us to go. We arrived to calls saying that she had developed bronchiolitis and was not expected to survive the night. The next day I was on the first flight out of Geneva. I remember praying that she would still be alive, because I could not bear the thought of not being with her when she died. Against all the odds, she pulled through and, contrary to early predictions, was very much aware that I was back with her.

I clearly remember the last week of Millie's life. I was really worried about her on the Monday morning school run. I took her to Helen House, in tears, saying she just wasn't right. Things got worse, and by Tuesday night we decided to take her to hospital. Millie was seriously ill, with bleeding and a dangerously low temperature as a result of a chest infection. We watched helplessly as our little daughter suffered a horrible illness. Despite Millie's frailty, her body refused to give in easily. Yet after a few days, it was obvious that she wasn't getting any better. The consultant talked us through the situation and suggested that it was time we transferred to Helen House. We had been dreading those words, as we knew that we would be taking Millie there for the last time. We arrived to a lovely welcome of tea and toast, hugs and tears. Millie was made comfortable in her bed. She was suddenly much more accessible, away from all the tubes and medical equipment. She visibly relaxed and even opened her eyes for the first time since her admission to hospital. Her brothers came to see her early the next morning before school. In true Millie fashion, she rallied noticeably in those last hours. We did not give up hope. But in the early hours of Saturday morning, four weeks to the hour after her sister Laura was born, Millie died. Death was a release, and when she died she looked radiant.

We have known God with us throughout this difficult journey. Our faith helped us to entrust Millie's life to God, to accept that he had a plan for her life and for our lives. When Millie died we had to give her back to God, which was incredibly painful because we wanted so much for her to stay with us, but at the same time we knew that death would release her from her suffering. However heartbreaking it was to say goodbye, Millie could now live life to the full in heaven. Our suffering does not go away, but Millie was a precious gift, and we are hugely grateful for her and for the time we spent with her.

This story was recently broadcast on BBC Radio 4 on *It's My Story: Remembering Millie.*[1]

1 If God exists, then why is there so much evil and suffering in the world?

'I'm sorry, there is nothing we can do for you.' The consultant's words confirmed what we already knew, but still they hung in the silence. Despite huge advances in modern medicine, most neurology patients still face the harsh reality that there is no cure for their illness. For some, this brings the devastating news of the beginning of the end of life, of staring mortality square in the face, perhaps for the first time. For my husband Conrad, there was no threat to life itself, only to its quality, but this wreaks havoc enough.

Yet we know we are not alone. We all have stories to tell. As the band R.E.M. put it two decades ago, 'Everybody hurts sometimes'. Pain and suffering are universal. No-one is exempt. Times of trouble and pain make us cry out for answers. Why, why, why?! If God exists, then why is there so much evil and suffering in the world?

As we begin to explore suffering, I would like to suggest that we need to start not with 'why?' but with 'if'. For the question of 'if' is crucial. In ancient Greece the Athenian king is known to have written a threatening letter to his city's arch-enemies in

Sparta, saying, 'You are advised to submit without further delay, for if I bring my army on your land, I will destroy your farms, slay your people and raze your city.' The Spartans, renowned for their military prowess but not their eloquence, responded with this one word: 'If'.

For Sparta, the question of 'if' was the difference between life and death, a bright future or a bitter end. So it is with God and suffering. The question of 'if' changes everything. For 'if' God exists, then he has some explaining to do, but 'if' he does not, then suffering is not a problem as such. Suffering is inconvenient, yes, distressing, yes, but problematic, no. For if there is no higher being and we are in a closed system, then to whom is your complaint being addressed?

'If' God exists, then he has some explaining to do, but 'if' he does not, then suffering is not a problem as such.

Our perspective on suffering is very much dependent on how we view the world. There are many different 'lenses' or religions available, each offering a different way to make sense of suffering. Many people think that deep down all religions are saying the same thing, even though they may appear superficially different. To help us decide, we need to dig beneath the surface and examine how the different major world religions each answer the question: 'If God exists, then why is there so much evil and suffering?'

Atheism

Atheism, taken from the Greek *a*: 'without', *theos*: 'God', is defined as 'the absence of belief in gods and the supernatural'.[1] It took root in revolutionary France when the middle classes rejected the oppressive state religion and it became a personally held belief in the nineteenth century. Today there are between 500 million and 750 million atheists worldwide.[2]

A key reason why atheists do not believe in God is the very existence of evil. If God were real, he would do something about it. Given that he has not done, then it is either certain[3] or highly probable[4] that God does not exist. Atheism solves the intellectual problem of evil by concluding that a world of pain is simply the way the world is. This then raises the question of how atheists define the very evil they abhor. In other words, how does one establish moral values, good and evil, right and wrong, without God? The majority of atheists agree that ethical codes of living are essential, but that human beings themselves are capable of devising them. The different approaches can be summarized as three main theories.

1. 'Each to their own'

The first theory deals with egoism, in which each person's own internal moral code determines what is right and wrong. We often hear this expressed in contemporary culture as, 'That's true for you but not true for me', or 'Each to their own', or 'You need to look out for number one'. The good is whatever is right for the individual, and the bad is whatever is not in his or her best interests. This is not just a recent phenomenon. The ancient Greek philosopher Protagoras claimed that 'Man is the measure of all things'.[5] On one level this is reasonable, and may work in the day-to-day decisions of, for example, what washing machine to buy or where to shop for our children's shoes. However, with more serious moral decision-making, we run into problems. What happens if an action taken in one person's interests harms another? Can you guarantee that people will always draw from their internal moral good? We cannot. A mere glance at the newspaper shows that we cannot guarantee that, in serving their own interests, people will also consider the interests of others.

The riots in London and other UK cities in August 2011 gave us an extreme snapshot of what society might look like if people were able to make their own rules. The cause of the riots was complex and involved more than just individuals acting selfishly. Nevertheless, it gave a glimpse of what could happen if the opportunity to create one's own morality is opened up. The nation looked on, stunned, as anarchy descended upon our capital city. Shops were ransacked and looted, cars set alight, and people were afraid to leave their homes for fear of attack or robbery. Opportunists cashed in. Thousands were doing it, and the police were powerless to stop it for a time. We saw communities of individuals each living by their own moral code. The result? Chaos.

A looter was interviewed shortly afterwards[6] and asked why he was stealing and looting. His reply was that there was an opportunity to get possessions free of charge and he wasn't going to miss it. It was as though he was perfectly justified in his actions. Yet when asked whether it would be acceptable for his own home to be looted, his response was one of outrage. That would be utterly unacceptable. This response to egoism is common. Whatever is right for us is fine until it literally 'comes knocking on our own door', and then (and sometimes only then) we are outraged and caused to invoke a higher moral standard that states that some things are universally wrong. The real world is clear that ethics centred on personal preference are simply unlivable, and those living in areas affected by the rioting would be the first to admit this.

2. The greater good

The second theory for establishing moral values is utilitarianism. In the late eighteenth and nineteenth centuries the philosophers and economists Jeremy Bentham and John Stuart Mill developed the theory that right actions are those that result in the greatest good for the greatest number of people, whereas wrong actions are those that tend to promote pain and harm. Actions are deemed right or wrong based on their consequences in the community, regardless of the initial motives or any good or bad within the act itself. In other words, *the ends justify the means*.

For example, the trafficking of African slaves to North America in the seventeenth century or indeed of young women to Europe in the twenty-first century would not necessarily be wrong according to utilitarianism. By the mid-nineteenth century, slavery was a thriving industry that bolstered the economy and crop production of fifteen states in the southern USA. Likewise, many profit financially and physically from the modern-day sex industry. Utilitarianism would assess whether human trafficking is right or wrong, based on outcomes. The process of assessing consequences is complex. Some utilitarians such as Peter Singer[7] would say that some 'rights' take precedence over others, for example the right to live overrides the right to business success. Many checks and balances are included and may generate a number of possible scenarios. The suffering of the slaves would certainly be taken into account, but if the benefits outweigh the harm of slavery itself, then an honest utilitarian would not have had grounds for the abolition that Wilberforce and others secured in 1807 or that anti-trafficking campaigners are pushing for today.

In practice, a number of problems arise. For how can people assess outcomes when we have such a limited perspective on life, may be biased about what is 'good' and cannot see very far into the future? Firstly, what is meant by a 'good' outcome? Bentham and Mill defined happiness as being intrinsically good, against which all other values were to be compared. Others have said our common sense would make the best outcome obvious. Therefore the definition of 'good' varies. Secondly, how does one define 'community' or 'the greatest number'? Thirdly, this ethic takes a diminished view of individuals. While communities are vital, does not the welfare of the individual matter too? Fourthly, how does one decide that the outcome of an action has run its course? To assess outcomes properly, a far bigger perspective is needed, arguably one that is outside of time and space itself. Fifthly, finally and most importantly, who should bear the responsibility for these decisions? For humans to evaluate outcomes that involve the lives and livelihoods of fellow human beings surely places undue pressure where it was never supposed to be.

3. Moral values have evolved

A third theory is that moral values have emerged through evolutionary mechanisms. J. H. Huxley and T. H. Huxley developed Darwin's biological theory of evolution into an ethic, stating that whatever aids the evolutionary process is right and whatever hinders it is wrong.[8] Over time, the environment, genetics and culture have shaped and refined social instincts such that the morally superior traits are those that enable the survival of the species.

There are some problems with this approach. Firstly, who or what decides what aids or hinders evolution? Some standard outside of the evolutionary process must be assumed, with the end-point in sight, as otherwise it would be impossible to define what progress actually is. Secondly, since there is no ultimate standard by which to measure progress, this quickly becomes a matter of subjective preference and switches into egoistic ethics. Even rape and murder could be justified in some circumstances, since they may help a person's own genes survive. Thirdly, sometimes conflicting instincts arise, and the prevailing one does not promote survival of the fittest. Take for example a mother who rescues her drowning baby, at great risk to her own life. The evolutionary 'good' would have been to save herself, for even a rescued baby with no mother to care for it would eventually die. Why then did another instinct overrule? Are all instincts equally valid? Or do humans behave as though some are more valid than others?

Richard Dawkins in his book *The Selfish Gene* sails evolutionary ethics full into the wind. Humans are mere pawns in the evolutionary process, whose sole function in life is to pass on their genetic material to the next generation. Jeffrey Skilling, the former CEO in the Enron scandal, was inspired by Dawkins and, in the words of one magazine, 'sought to apply nature's lessons to the energy industry'. The working environment was brutal. 'Skilling . . . implemented a system known as "rank and yank" that . . . had all employees in the company ranked every six months. Then he offered lavish bonuses to the top 5 percent while the bottom 15 percent were relocated or fired.'[9] On hearing this, Dawkins was said to have been appalled, commenting that the emphasis of his book was intended to be upon 'gene' rather than 'selfish', and translating genetic behaviour into business ethics was a step too far. Yet in the absence of a transcendent standard, who decides? How ironic that Enron is now extinct.

This outworking of evolutionary ethics is dark, but it gets darker still. The Nazi leader Adolf Hitler in his book *Mein Kampf* (1925) worked out a form of social Darwinism. He extrapolated the principles of natural selection and survival of the fittest to ethnic groups, in order to preserve what he viewed as 'stronger' (Aryan) races, and remove 'weaker' (Jewish and other non-Aryan) ones. Of course, it is essential to add here that the vast majority of people who would claim their morality has evolved would not dream of taking things to such extremes. The morality of many who do not believe in God can often put to shame that of those of us who do. However, a crucial question to ask is: 'What sorts of things become *permissible* if God does not exist and human beings are at the helm?' If the only moral law is the internal one within, or is determined by evolution, then whether we are in a classroom or a death camp, anything goes, and it doesn't matter who gets hurt. If God does not exist, then people can justifiably make up their own rules.

So we have seen three of the ways in which right and wrong are defined in the absence of God. Moral values are defined in terms of personal preference (egoism), the best outcome for the greatest number of people (utilitarianism) or survival instincts (evolutionary ethics). Although these theories each highlight aspects of right and wrong that may contribute towards an ultimate definition of right and wrong, in and of themselves they are unlivable. So what answers do the other world faiths offer?

Hinduism

There are 800 million Hindus in the world, comprising 13% of the world's population. In broad terms, Hindus worship either many finite gods (polytheistic Hinduism; derived from *polus*: 'many'; *theos*: 'god') or one infinite God (pantheistic Hinduism; derived from *pan*: 'all'; *theos*: 'god') or a combination of the two.

In the polytheistic form of Hinduism, the good and evil we encounter in life are a result of the ongoing battle between up to 330 million gods, some of whom are good, others evil. In the pantheistic form, good and evil belong to the lower-level physical world of illusion (*maya*), and must be transcended into a higher spiritual reality known as Brahman, which is beyond such categories, i.e. beyond good and evil.

Brahman is infinite but impersonal, and is better described as 'it' rather than 'he' or 'she'. Therefore there is no 'being' as such to whom to address our 'why?' question. Humans are extensions of Brahman – if you like, mini-gods – because the essence of pantheism is that all is God and God is all. Upright living is an intrinsic part of the journey, and virtues such as truthfulness, love and good judgment are highly esteemed, but must eventually be discarded as higher and higher levels are attained. In order to merge with Brahman, the pantheist must let go of the concern of morality and pass beyond good and evil, since that is where God is. As Prabhavananda puts it, 'If we say, "I am good," or "I am bad," we are only talking the language of maya (the world of illusion). "I am Brahman," is the only true statement regarding ourselves that any of us can make.'[10]

This approach appears peaceable but has huge implications. If evil is not real, then why does it seem to scream at us so loudly from our streets, our schools, our TV screens and our households?

If evil is illusory, then why would anyone lock their door at night? Is it really possible to live as though there is no difference between love and murder, generosity and theft, disease and health? The philosopher Francis Schaeffer proposed that, if a belief system is true, then it is also fully livable for anyone, in any culture, in any demographic group, at any time point in history. If at any point our beliefs have to be suspended in order to continue living, then the truth of those beliefs is called into question. Equally, to what belief system has one defaulted in order to continue living? Schaeffer illustrates the point with this story:

> One day I was talking to a group of people in the digs of a young South African in Cambridge. Among others, there was present a young Indian who was of Sikh background but a Hindu by religion. He started to speak strongly against Christianity, but did not really understand the problems of his own beliefs. So I said, 'Am I not correct in saying that on the basis of your system, cruelty and non-cruelty are ultimately equal, that there is no intrinsic difference between them?' He agreed . . . The student in whose room we met, who had clearly understood the implications of what the Sikh had admitted, picked up his kettle of boiling water with which he was about to make tea, and stood with it steaming over the Indian's head. The man looked up and asked him what he was doing and he said with a cold yet gentle finality, 'There is no difference between cruelty and non-cruelty.' Thereupon the Hindu walked out into the night.[11]

The question of whether this young man could *live* what he *believed* revealed a stark inconsistency.

Buddhism

Buddhism was born out of Hinduism and out of a desire to acknowledge that evil and suffering are real. The Buddha or 'the enlightened one' was born as Prince Siddhartha Gautama between 624 and 563 BC in present-day Nepal. As part of a wealthy family with a protective father, he led a pampered life within the confines of the palatial home. As an adult, he finally ventured out, only to be shocked by the sickness and death he encountered.

At the age of twenty-nine, with much heartache, the disillusioned prince left his wife and baby boy to wander through the plains of eastern India in search of the truth, and is said to have reached enlightenment seven years later. After a further two months he delivered his first sermon and introduced the world to the Four Noble Truths that were to change the course of Asian history. The first Noble Truth establishes the human problem: life is fraught with affliction and suffering (*dukkha*) at every turn. The second Noble Truth diagnoses that the cause of suffering is craving (*tanha*), desire or attachment to the world. The third Noble Truth prescribes that suffering can be overcome by extinguishing desire. The fourth Noble Truth offers that the way to extinguish desire is via the Eightfold Path, which involves emotional, mental and physical exercises aimed at perfecting right view, right resolve, right speech, right action, right livelihood, right effort, right mindfulness and right concentration.[12] Progress along this path eventually leads to *nirvana*, an enlightened state bringing the cessation of desire, detachment from the world and suffering, and liberation from the cycle of birth and rebirth of which each person is a part.

Buddhism then acknowledges evil, but the solution is not to challenge it but to detach oneself from it. The final state of nirvana (meaning 'nothingness' or 'extinction') is one in which the individual is extinguished along with their desires. It is ultimately impersonal and therefore bears many similarities to pantheistic Hinduism. The apologist Os Guinness puts it well:

> To say it again, in the Buddhist view there is quite simply no remedy for suffering in this world. Nor is there any prospect of

a coming world without suffering. There is not even the hope that you and I will ever live free of suffering. And finally, there is no 'you' or 'I' at all . . . There is only the nobility of the compassion of the enlightened on their road to the 'liberation' of extinction.[13]

Buddhism engages with the reality of evil and suffering. But the proposed solution is problematic, since the ultimate goal is self-refuting. Extinguishing desire is itself a desire, therefore why would you wish to remove it?

Islam

Islam is one of the monotheistic (from *mono*: 'one', and *theos*: 'god') religions that believe in one all-encompassing God. It means 'submission', and Muslims or 'submitted ones' are numbered at over a billion, comprising a fifth of the world's population. The founder, Muhammad, an Arabian trader from Mecca born in AD 570, received a series of visions over a fifteen-year period that were taken to be the final revelation of God. After his death in AD 632 these visions were recorded to form the Qur'an.

Muslims believe in one God, Allah, who created and sustains the whole universe. They also believe that real evil exists, which at times is personified as Satan, and at other times is a more impersonal 'principle of evil'. Two main themes are emphasized regarding evil and suffering. Firstly, humans are created to worship God, but are tempted to go astray by Satan and their own desires. However, every person has an inner capacity to resist temptation and ought to succeed with the help of angels and messengers sent from Allah. Secondly, all events that come to pass, both good and bad, are considered to be the will of Allah. A phrase frequently uttered in the Islamic world is *inshallah*, which means 'if God wills'; in other words, 'If you are healthy it is that God wishes you to be so, therefore be grateful. If you suffer, God wishes to test you.'[14] The appropriate response to suffering in Islam is to accept the will of God.

Christianity

Christianity is viewed by many in Western Europe as a dying religion. They have either had it forced down their throats as children, and consequently rejected it as adults, or have grown up oblivious and are happy to continue without it. Some may pay homage at Christmas and Easter, weddings and christenings, but even these are being replaced with late-night shopping, hotel wedding services and child-naming ceremonies.

Christianity faces the problem of evil head-on.

When we revisit church for these rites of passage our childhood hymns are brought out. A cultural favourite: 'All Things Bright and Beautiful' parodies how many perceive the Christian God: a god who created a beautiful world long ago but doesn't seem to do much today. At best he tinkers around the edges of our lives, making things a little better sometimes. As the Tesco slogan says, 'Every little helps', and Christianity as a little addition to life is no exception.

Yet this could not be further from the truth. Christianity faces the problem of evil head-on. It is the only belief system in which evil is a *problem* as such, because Christians do not deny the existence of God as atheists do, nor do they deny the existence of evil as pantheists do, nor do they deny the power of one supreme God as polytheists do, nor do they accept the will of God as Muslims do. Rather, Christians hold that a God exists who is fully good, fully loving and fully powerful, but that real evil also exists. At first glance these tenets appear contradictory, and therefore philosophers have developed reasons why this kind of God might also allow suffering. The term given to this is 'theodicy', a term originally coined by the eighteenth-century German philosopher Gottfried Leibniz.[15] It is derived from the Greek *theos* meaning 'god' and *dike* meaning 'justice', and it literally means, 'the justice of God'.

This is not the way things are supposed to be

My husband's illness began at the age of eleven with a bang to the head, and what developed shortly afterwards is still not fully understood by neurologists. The pattern has been that years and years of full health are interspersed with periods of illness that range in severity from being unable to work to being unable to walk or speak as well. These periods recurred when Conrad was fifteen for four months, and in his mid-twenties for fourteen months while studying for a PhD. I met Conrad shortly after his recovery from this prolonged time of illness. While we were dating we discovered that cranial osteopathy, a method of manipulating the head, could reverse the symptoms. While not understanding why this should work, we were obviously grateful for a treatment that could restore full health. In eleven years of married life Conrad has been ill a further four times, and some of our biggest challenges have involved coping with it as a family of four, as we now have two children.

During times of illness there is a definite impact on family life. It is impossible to predict what each day will hold, and so making plans is very difficult. A marker of how we are doing is whether or not we manage as a family to go swimming on Saturday mornings and then pile into a coffee shop afterwards. Such a simple thing ought not to make such a difference, and yet it does. On the weeks when we are not able to go I am especially prone to asking, 'Why can't I just have a normal life? Why can't we just manage to do the things that are so basic for other families?' But then the question comes hot on its heels: What exactly *is* a 'normal' life? And why is it that times of suffering invoke such a strong desire for it?

This cry for normality becomes louder when the suffering moves from bad to horrendous. When loved ones are raped and murdered, our inner scream is: 'This is not the way things are supposed to be!' Some may deny the existence of evil in the lecture theatre, but few can deny it when their loved one is fighting for their life in the operating theatre. This is *not* the way things were supposed to be.

But if we allow full vent to our outrage that 'this is not the way things were supposed to be', this begs a second question: 'How exactly are things supposed to be then?' It is as though, when face to face with suffering, we become aware of not just one standard, but two. Firstly, how things actually are but we wish they weren't, and secondly, how we would like things to be but they aren't.

Many have concluded that the existence of evil must be evidence against the existence of God, when in fact it could be evidence *for* his existence. The question: 'Why can't I have a normal life?' evokes memories of the days when we did have one. The Saturdays that are bereft of family swimming are painful because I remember the times when it was possible. Looting and rioting create outrage because just days previously the streets were peaceful and the shops intact. Cancer is able to spread because it corrupts and feeds off healthy cells. Rape is such an abomination because it is sex reduced to lust and raw mechanics.

Evil and the suffering it wreaks do not purely exist as a first cause. It is good that has been corrupted, and our sense of outrage and anger at evil shows that we identify evil precisely by contrasting it with good. While Buddha's first Noble Truth acknowledges that suffering is real, is it really true that the *whole of life* is suffering? Could it be that the deprivation and death that he saw were so stark because he had lived a privileged life until that point? Could it be that he needed the 'good' in order to recognize the bad?

Augustine of Hippo described evil as a privation or corruption of the good.[16] Evil is an absence of good that is understood only in relation to its first cause: good. Theologians and philosophers down the ages and today have used this to argue from the existence of evil to the existence of God. If real evil exists, which most are persuaded it does, then real good must also exist, because the recognition of evil is dependent on good. Therefore absolute moral standards, or a moral law, exist. What is the most likely origin of such a moral law? A moral lawgiver who epitomizes the ultimate standard of goodness. In other words, a God who is ultimately and completely good in character and actions, against whom all other standards of good and evil are compared. The apologist Ravi Zacharias describes an interaction with a student at Nottingham University on this topic:

> As soon as I finished one of my lectures [the student] shot up from his seat and blurted out rather angrily, 'There is too much evil in this world; therefore, there cannot be a God.' I asked him to remain standing and answer a few questions for me. I said, 'If there is such a thing as evil, aren't you assuming there is such a thing as good?' He paused, reflected, and said, 'I guess so.' 'If there is such a thing as good,' I countered, 'you must affirm a moral law on the basis of which to differentiate between good and evil.' . . . 'When you say there is evil, aren't you admitting there is good? When you accept the existence of goodness, you must affirm a moral law on the basis of which to differentiate between good and evil. But when you admit to a moral law, you must posit a moral lawgiver. That, however, is who you are trying to disprove and not prove. For if there is no moral lawgiver, there is no moral law. If there is no moral law, there is no good. If there is no good, there is no evil. What then is your question?' There was a conspicuous pause that was broken when he said rather sheepishly, 'What then am I asking you?' There's the rub, I might add.[17]

The existence of evil is not categorical evidence against God; in fact it could well be evidence for him. Instead of crying out, 'This is not the way things are supposed to be!', we could cry, 'Focus on higher things!' or 'This is *precisely* the way things are supposed to be!' or 'Why wouldn't things be this way?' Yet, acknowledging that evil is wrong but real seems to be our instinctive response. Theism, and within it Christianity, uniquely says that our instincts are correct. Evil exists because the enemy of God, Satan, also exists and is behind the atrocities of this world. Yet it is important to add that good and evil are not fighting it out in a battle of equals. God is greater than Satan, something we will discuss further in chapter 6.

Once again this does not provide us with all of the answers, but, as Ravi Zacharias has pointed out, there is a difference between a worldview that offers some but not complete answers, and a worldview that offers no answers or contradictory answers, or asks you to deny the emotions of grief, anger and sorrow that seem so very real.

If God exists, why is there so much evil and suffering in the world? I would argue that the existence of evil gives evidence of a good, moral lawgiver: God. But you, the reader, must decide.

2 If God knew the world would be a place of suffering, then why did he create it?

For some time now scientists have been trying to recreate the conditions at the beginning of the universe. The hope is that one day there will be data to verify M-theory,[1] an all-encompassing theory that explains the entire universe and how it began. Yet Stephen Hawking, one of M-theory's proponents, has himself admitted in the past that even physics cannot answer every question, because 'you still have the question: why does the universe bother to exist?'[2]

Although initially voiced as a scientific enquiry, this question intensifies in the light of the suffering on our planet. Even if we were to give some credence to the possibility of God's existence, then another difficult question arises: Surely if God exists, had the power to create a universe and knew that life would involve suffering, then why did he bother creating anything in the first place? Doesn't it seem somewhat sadistic to force humans into existence and inflict upon them a life of suffering and pain, and yet offer them no choice over whether they should exist or not? Humans did not choose to exist. Perhaps it would have been better for God not to have created life at all?

Is God immoral?

As we saw at the end of the last chapter, merely asking, 'Why did God create a suffering world?' invokes moral standards and applies them to God. In other words, if the decision and capability to create were in God's hands, and he knew that people would suffer as a result, then surely it was immoral or questionable of him to introduce suffering when he had the option to avoid it altogether? In other words, it is inferred that there are acceptable and unacceptable standards of conduct regarding the creation of universes, to which even God must answer. If these standards exist, then the question stands, but if they do not, then the question is void. So which is it?

Interestingly, as my colleague Michael Ramsden points out, the majority of the complaints that people have about God refer to his moral character.[3] In this case, if God had the power to withhold unnecessary suffering from humankind but didn't, what does this say about him? Does the needless pain of helpless people bring him pleasure? Is he some sort of divine sadist or torturer? Did he fling the universe into existence, caring nothing for the consequences?

In the beginning . . .

As part of our journey it is worth seeing how the different religions account for the creative process. Since atheists do not believe that God exists, there is no being involved in the origins of the universe. Matter explains everything. Either matter has always existed and the universe was created *ex materia*, out of pre-existing matter, or matter spontaneously came into existence out of nothing. But there was no *decision* as such involved in creation, merely chance. Under atheism, there is no 'being' to whom we can direct outrage or a sense of injustice.

Eastern thought varies on beginnings. For some, the natural world is considered *maya* or illusion, and only exists in the sense of coming 'out of god the way a dream comes from a mind'.[4] In this case, the question is a distraction from higher things. Others would say that the universe was created *ex Deo*, or 'out of God'. In other words, God is the created world, and the created world is God. Therefore the universe exists out of necessity because it is purely an extension of the Divine. Though the route is different, the destination is the same as for atheism: there was no decision as such to create, and therefore a justification for the creative act is not needed. The universe simply is.

Theists believe that the universe was created out of nothing (*ex nihilo*) by a God who has imprinted himself upon nature, and yet at the same time has remained distinct from it. The universe was not started by chance nor necessity, nor to meet a need within God, but as a decision, and it is to this God that our question, 'Why bother creating anything?', still stands.

Existence or non-existence?

So let's address the question to the theistic God: 'Why bother creating a world at all?' An honest starting point is to say that this is difficult to answer from within time and space. Buried beneath the question is the possibility that non-existence might be preferable to existence. Yet we have only known what it is to exist, and therefore how can we comment on non-existence? The children's author and apologist C. S. Lewis puts it well:

> I must warn the reader that I shall not attempt to prove that to create was better than not to create: I am aware of no human scales in which such a portentous question can be weighed. Some comparison between one state of being and another can be made, but the attempt to compare being and not being ends

in mere words. 'It would be better for me not to exist' – in what sense 'for me'? How should I, if I did not exist, profit by not existing?[5]

Instead we can ask another question: Is this life all bad? Yes, there is suffering in our world, but is that all there is to life? The aim here is not to trivialize the tragedy that befalls people, but simply to ask the question: Is there still anything, or has there ever been anything, worth getting out of bed for each morning? Could there ever be anything again in the future? Before, after or on the day your life fell apart? Is there anything to be thankful for in life, even in the midst of difficulties? If the answer to any of these questions is 'yes', then existence remains a valid option. We must remember that non-existence would withhold all of the good as well as the bad.

Does the bad really outweigh the good?

Some people's personal suffering is so all-consuming that it is hard for them to recall happy memories or see anything worth living for. Yet when we consider the entire human race throughout human history, can we confidently conclude that the bad outweighs the good? Again we have raised a question that is impossible to answer, because it requires a completely objective survey of the total amount of good and evil in the world across the whole of human history. We are inside of time and space and therefore not in a position to make such an assessment.

Furthermore, the media have decided that what constitutes 'news' is mostly 'bad news'. Our newspapers, TV news programmes and radio broadcasts are full of robberies, attacks on people, deaths of the famous, child abuse, and so the list goes on. Occasionally at the end of a broadcast we are treated to a more encouraging story, but much of the time we are bombarded and overwhelmed by the suffering of others. As a result, who could blame anyone for asking, 'Why did God bother creating a suffering world?'

But have the media got it right or are they only presenting half of the story? I have heard of and wept over children I have known who have died in infancy, and yet I also know that at the hospital not one mile from my front door hundreds of healthy babies are born every year and live to become adults. We hear daily of children and adults on the brink of starvation, and yet millions have plenty to eat. We hear of those who have been maimed and scarred by war, unable to rest because of constant fear of danger, and yet we also know of the many who sleep soundly every night in a safe, warm, dry house. We hear of deadly diseases, and yet also know that scientific research has produced vaccinations that can prevent many of them.

So for the human race as a whole, is it all bad news? Or is there much that does indeed make life worth living? While we can't assess whether it might have been better not to exist, is there not much to our existence that we can enjoy and be thankful for? Even if the bad does outweigh the good, does it mean that the good wasn't worth it? Does it mean that relationships that we are given for a time weren't worth it? Such is the impact of love that even some who have experienced great personal loss would still echo the words of Tennyson:

'Tis better to have loved and lost
Than never to have loved at all.[6]

Early in our marriage Conrad and I enjoyed a three-year period in the USA. When the time came to move back to the UK we made a thorough search for a low-cost shipping company, packed up our possessions and had them sent off ahead of us. Around six weeks later we were beginning to grow concerned, since there was no word of our shipment and calls were not being returned. Eventually we discovered that our possessions were still sitting in a crate 10 miles from our former US home and being held to ransom by the shipping company. The cost of the shipment had sharply increased and the goods would not be released unless a higher price was paid. The US Maritime Commission became involved and helped us get our belongings back, but not without cost in terms of time and money. When the fate of our shipment was still uncertain, I remember discussing what we would miss most if we never saw any of our possessions again. Photos and sentimental items would have been our biggest loss. Why? Because they hold memories of relationships with both friends and family, memories that would be lost because life had moved on. They were unique and irreplaceable.

While we can't even begin to answer the 'why?' of many people's suffering, sometimes our inbuilt need for relationships points us in the right direction. On a larger scale, could it be that God allowed humankind to exist, because our existence, even though painful and at times marked with tragedy, allowed the possibility of irreplaceable relationships? Relationships that are not restricted to the domain of romance, but that also include friendships, bonds between siblings, the protective love of parents for their children, and so on. Are we not driven and defined by relationships? Do we not often check and post messages on our email or Facebook or Twitter before we eat breakfast or even surface from bed? We want – we need – relationships. Where does this relationality come from?

Could it be that it was better to exist than not, because by existing, the possibility of a life-changing and unending relationship with our Creator is made possible? This may be the beginnings of an answer to why God created something rather than nothing. But it leads to another question: Couldn't God have created a *better* world? We'll look at this in our next chapter.

Will's story

We'd been married since 1988, I was enjoying a career in the army, and Anna and I were really happy and fulfilled. In fact, people used to refer to us as the 'Ski family' because we resembled the family of four that advertised Ski yoghurts on TV.

The day my world fell apart was a gloriously hot summer's day. Anna was driving back from a trip to the beach with our three-year-old daughter Eleanor and two-year-old son Jamie. For some unknown reason, her car strayed over the centre of the road and hit an oncoming 40-ton articulated lorry. Both were travelling at about 45 mph, so it was like hitting a brick wall at 90 mph. Anna and Jamie died instantly. Eleanor survived unscathed and was pulled from the wreckage by the driver of the car behind. I was at work some 70 miles away. I shall never forget that hot July evening, being driven by two police officers from Camberley to Salisbury to identify Anna and Jamie's mangled bodies. As we drove into the setting sun, I remember thinking that my life was never going to be the same again.

They took me to the hospital. A policeman ushered me into the mortuary, a very clinical white room. There was an adult draped in a white sheet and a little tea trolley concealing something much smaller. The officer lifted the white sheet. I saw Anna's face and just broke down. I didn't really want to touch her. They'd obviously tried to wash the blood out of her hair, but with little success, and her face was misshapen. Then the officer moved the sheet from my little boy, and it was like he was asleep, with a cut under one eye. I couldn't believe that this small boy who had been such a handful, this little dynamo of energy, was now cold and lifeless. I touched his cheek but it was stone cold. I cried out, I sobbed, I wept, and thought to myself that this isn't them. You can't just extinguish two such vital and energy-filled people. This can't be the end for them; they must be somewhere else. It occurred to me that what I was looking at was just like a shell you find on a beach, a shell that had once housed a precious life that is no longer there. In the fluorescent glare of the room something drew my eyes to a simple wooden crucifix on one of the bare walls. Such a familiar symbol after the drip, drip, drip of Christian teaching at school which I found so boring and irrelevant. I looked at this cross, and something seemed to fall into place. I knew in an instant that it was going to be a sign of hope for me.

I went back to the police station to collect my little girl. She was a complete miracle, with just a slight bruise where the seat belt had cut into her. She was absolutely fine. I told her that Mummy and Jamie were gone and that we weren't going to see them any more. At that time *The Lion King* was my children's favourite film, and Eleanor asked me, 'Have Mummy and Jamie gone to be stars in the sky?'

'Yes, they have,' I said.

I took her home, and the days passed in a haze. I lost a stone in weight in a week. But I remember walking the dog up and down outside our house, looking at the stars in the sky one beautiful July night and wondering, 'Why am I still holding it together?' People kept on saying, 'We are praying for you.' I received lots of cards about God and Jesus loving us, and was very conscious that what was keeping me going might well be people's prayers.

I helped to dig their grave, which was a cathartic experience, and the funeral passed in a blur. Days came when I ranted and shouted at God. 'Why, God? Why? Why did you let this happen? They were so perfect, so lovely, so wonderful. If you're the big God of love and mercy, why didn't you just save them? You could have done it! You parted the Red Sea! You raised people from the dead! You changed water into wine! Why couldn't you just have touched that steering wheel and stopped the collision happening?' I called God names. I told him exactly what I thought of him.

I had had everything I could possibly desire. A good job, a lovely family and enough money, but when so much of such importance was torn away from me, I needed to look outside of myself for answers. Material things had let me down, shown to be only transitory. I needed to know where my family were, who was looking after them, and, if they were in heaven, what I needed to do to make sure I ended up in the same place. I suppose in a military sense my mission was to make sure I was going there as well. I was told that Christians believed that to get to heaven you need to have a personal relationship with Jesus Christ, and so I said 'OK, that's fine; how do I have a personal relationship with Jesus Christ?' In the coming weeks and months I looked into the Christian faith. Over time, and by reading the Bible, I became captivated by this person, Jesus, this incredible teacher, this miracle worker, this man who experienced everything we experience in this life, and more: death, bereavement, pain, joy, happiness. I thought that the evidence for the existence of Jesus Christ and the evidence for his claims to be God all stacked up. I realized that I needed to make a decision, and it seemed a bit of a no-brainer, but at that time it was a decision in my head. Then I found a strange sense of peace as I began to accept Jesus into my life. I started to pray, and prayers seemed to get answered. Two or three years later something else also fell into place in my heart. I found myself in a church, the likes of which I'd never been in before and didn't even know existed. Here was a place that was absolutely alive. One evening during a sermon on sin I found myself shaking and weeping uncontrollably, which, for someone who has been in the army, a pretty stiff-upper-lip sort of guy, was a very alarming experience. I asked the person next to me to explain what was happening. They said that the Holy Spirit was at work, and it was from that moment onwards that I began to be aware of the power of the Holy Spirit, and my life really started to change.

Little Eleanor was doing remarkably well and seemed to understand where her mummy and brother were. Her childlike imagination of God served her well, as she was able to picture them both in God's loving hands. A couple of years after the accident when we were alone together, Eleanor asked me a question: 'Daddy, God is huge, isn't he? He has the whole world in his hands, doesn't he?'

'Yes,' I replied, pleased that she was absorbing the Christian message.

'God really loves us, doesn't he, Daddy?'

'Yes,' I replied, 'he loves us a huge, huge, huge amount.'

'Nothing is impossible for God, is it?' she persisted. I was starting to wonder where her line of questioning was leading when she asked the final question: 'So if God can do anything and he loves us a huge, huge, huge amount, then why did he let Mummy's car hit the lorry? Why didn't he just reach down and stop the accident happening?'

I was so shocked, so dumbstruck, that I am not sure how long it took me to compose myself. I had ranted at God, shouted at him so many tear-filled times. But now this precious child of mine, with no anger, no name-calling, was gently asking the same question.

I don't know how I would have coped without God. I was in a group with others who had lost children, and so many were very, very bitter, unable to forgive and therefore unable to move forward. Knowing I am forgiven by God has released me to forgive others. I have been able to forgive the lorry driver. I have been able to forgive my wife and, through that forgiveness, look forward to a new start in life without emotional baggage. I was able to trust that God was with me. I was able to talk to him through prayer and I saw many prayers answered. I had some big decisions to make and was able to talk to him about those decisions. Some I got right; some I didn't. Some, looking back, he warned me about, but I closed my ears to him and ended up making mistakes. Even so, I was very aware of the constant presence of God in my life. People used to say, 'Eleanor has grown up wonderfully. Gosh, you're so lucky', and I would reply, 'It's nothing to do with luck; it's because people are praying for her.' I had prayed over her every single night.

Almost ten years ago now I met and married Lucia, also a Christian, and we enjoy a wonderful marriage. We had two beautiful girls together and were going to stop there because of difficult births, but we both really wanted a third child. On our wedding anniversary Lucia was praying and sensed that God was saying to her, 'Have another child. It will be OK.' We decided to try, and it was a boy. I feel like the character, Job, in the Bible, who had so much taken away from him, but then was restored with much more than he had started out with. One of our girls is called Jemima, the name of one of Job's daughters after he was restored. The boy? His name is Theodore which means 'gift of God', and this sums it all up. He is, plainly and simply, a gift from God.

3 If God is so powerful, then why doesn't he stop evil before it happens?

In 1938 Superman made his debut into comic books. He was exactly what his name suggested: outwardly a normal-looking man, yet with superhuman abilities and a protector of the public. Since this original superhero, Batman, Spiderman, Captain America, Iron Man and many others with superhuman status have been created. In each story the heroes use their powers to prevent a whole range of catastrophes and ultimately defeat their evil opponents. This is the assumed and accepted outcome of a superhero storyline, since the evil use of power would not merit the term 'hero'. This thinking carries over from comic books into real life and to how we think about God. Many assume that if someone were given unlimited power, then surely they would use it to stop evil every time? Moreover, if God is both good and powerful, why doesn't he put on his metaphorical cloak of power, play the superhero and stop evil before it happens?

In the last chapter we considered why God was justified in creating any world as opposed to nothing at all. Now we'll ask, 'Why could God not have created a *better* world?' A better world in which people do not die in their prime, nor catch terrible diseases, nor experience betrayal by their closest friends, nor have to bury their children. Is ours really the best possible world we could have? The French philosopher Voltaire sarcastically asked in *Candide*, 'If this is the best of all possible worlds then what are the others like?'[1]

In answering the question: 'If God is so powerful, then why doesn't he stop evil before it happens?', all of the reasons in this chapter on their own will be insufficient. Why God might intervene to stop certain evils but permit others, especially horrendous and gratuitous ones, has an element of mystery to it that any apologist would be a fool not to acknowledge. Will's daughter asked a question that probes these very depths. Why couldn't God have moved the lorry a few more centimetres across the road? That wouldn't have impeded anyone's freedom and would have made for a better world, certainly for a girl and her mother. Any answers need to be sufficient for a four-year-old who experienced grief before she learned how to spell the word.

Powerful and loving?

Buried within this question lie more questions about the character of God. In other words, by asking the question we state that there are acceptable and unacceptable standards concerning the type of world God could have created. Given that God has created an apparently faulty world, yet was powerful enough to do otherwise, what does this say about him? Some recent films have featured superheroes that fall short of their capabilities. Will Smith in *Hancock* plays a superhero with attitude. He is capable of good but prefers to behave like a rebellious teenager. How one uses power speaks volumes about their moral character, and therefore we cannot examine God's power without also examining the extent to which he loves.

The question: 'If God is so powerful, then why doesn't he stop evil before it happens?' is uniquely problematic for the Christian God who claims to be all-powerful (omnipotent), all-loving (benevolent) and yet intimately concerned with the lives of individuals (omniscient). But surely an all-powerful, all-loving God would not tolerate pointless and gratuitous evil, and would stop it before it happens? Given that he does not, then we are left with a number of alternatives. Firstly, perhaps God is more akin to the enemies of Superman, Spiderman and Batman, and prefers to use his power for harm and destruction? In other words, he is malevolent and does not stop evil because he is the cause of it. Secondly, perhaps he has a split personality and uses his power for good in one moment and evil the next, and therefore cannot be relied upon? Thirdly, perhaps he resembles Hancock and is perfectly capable of stopping evil but is immature, lazy or neglectful or simply has favourites? Fourthly, perhaps he is not all-powerful, but a faded old man who watches helplessly as the events of the world spiral out of control? In short, God must be malevolent, volatile, indifferent or helpless. Some may find it easier to be reconciled to a God who would dearly love to stop evil, but sadly cannot do anything about it, rather than a God who is able to deal with evil but chooses not to do so.

So why does a loving, powerful God not stop every evil before it happens? People have wrestled with these questions for centuries. Some philosophers suggest that God permits evil not because of a lack of love, nor a misuse of power, but because he has sufficient reasons for doing so. But what might those reasons be?

Alternative worlds

Imagine for a moment that you are God and have been assigned the task of creating a new world. Such things are not difficult to conceive of in today's culture where we dip in and out of other worlds through video games and the 3D virtual world of Second Life.[2] In this task you are given just one thing to uphold: that this new world must be as loving and moral as it could possibly be. So how would you organize everything? How would you set up the natural world and its laws? Would you include water, without which life cannot exist and yet with which there is the possibility of drowning? Would you exclude bacteria, thereby ruling out MRSA and other fatal diseases but also impeding the digestive process of every living creature? Would you allow people to feel physical pain, without which they might be oblivious to health problems? What sort of nature would you give people? Would you allow them advanced cognitive abilities, knowing that they could invent technologies and medicines that save billions of lives but also weapons that could wipe out life? Would you make them selfless or selfish, or both? We don't have to ponder the idea for long before realizing that creating a perfect world is not as straightforward as we might think.

Creating a perfect world is not as straightforward as we might think.

There are many alternative types of world that could have been created. Considering all the possibilities is beyond the scope of this book, but we will look at three. Would any of these worlds be better and more moral than the one we already have, in which real moral freedom and real evil exist in parallel?

1. A non-free world

One possibility is to create a world in which people know they are not free, in which God constantly overrules decisions and choices, so that people always choose the good and the right. What would society look like in such a world? We might be grateful for safe flights, safe children and safe streets, but how would this be accomplished? Would the pen of the person cheating in an exam always fail to write? Would the words of slander or rage fail to come out of every mouth or else fall on deaf ears? Perhaps every gun would jam before it could fire the fatal shot? Perhaps every knife would fail to puncture the skin? What about thoughts? Would they be overruled too? Frankly, it is hard to imagine this hypothetical world. Perhaps much evil would be prevented, but the inability to make any form of meaningful decision might itself lead to meaninglessness and despair, and contempt for the God who treats people like puppets or pieces on a chessboard.

Many in the workplace complain of being micro- or line-managed. Often this term is used in a derogatory way to describe bosses who intervene too much and disempower their employees. The employee then feels hassled, unimportant and irrelevant, and may even ask the question, 'Why am I here?' Micro-managing leads to exasperation and frustration. Such a method is generally considered unethical in the workplace. Why then would we be prepared to attribute an unethical use of power to God? A world in which people are knowingly prevented from making real choices is a possible world, but also an immoral one.

2. A world with the appearance of freedom

A second option is to create a world with the appearance of freedom. The movie *The Truman Show* gave us a glimpse into such a world. The lead character, Truman Burbank, is a salesman oblivious to the fact that his life is a TV show watched by millions. His home town of Seahaven is a gigantic film set; he thinks he is married to Meryl but she is fictional, and the insurance company he thinks he works for does not in fact exist. Everyone else is in on the deal except Truman himself, and the film strapline: 'On the air. Unaware' summarizes it well. The movie ends with Truman leaving home to broaden his horizons, only to discover that those horizons are made of canvas. He discovers the truth about his captivity and escapes into real freedom. The movie is clear that true freedom for Truman is the only morally right outcome. This truth carries over into real life. A world with the appearance of freedom or false freedom is a morally inferior option, violating something of our humanity. Why? Because hiding the truth requires dishonesty and deception.

Is not flawed freedom better than false freedom or no freedom at all? Is not choice one of the greatest dignities that can be given to a human being? Is not discrimination unjust, precisely because it removes from people's lives the ability to choose? Is not poverty debilitating because it imposes a limited standard of living and also removes the ability to choose for oneself and one's family? When living on the poverty line you do not have a choice about whether or not to feed your children healthy food; you simply have to buy the cheapest available. Some have no choice about whether or not to move into the catchment of a school with a good reputation. The catchment area corresponding to the housing you can afford is the only option. In parts of the developing world it can be hard to access medical care, because the nearest hospital is unaffordable or several hours' drive away. Therefore you have your baby at home, in full knowledge that if there are complications, then there is no emergency C-section, and death in childbirth is a very real possibility for both mother and baby. Real freedom to choose is the ultimate dignity that a person can have, and its absence can sometimes mean the difference between life and death.

3. A free world in which people always choose good

A third possibility is to create a free world, but one in which no-one commits evil. In other words, freedom is real, but people are guaranteed always to choose the good. The problem is that a world with morally significant freedom is a world in which good decisions cannot be guaranteed, because moral freedom requires that good and bad options are both freely available. We assume that if God is all-powerful, then he can do absolutely everything that it is possible to do. But even an omnipotent God cannot guarantee that good decisions will be made by free people. He cannot both consistently assign free will and consistently withhold it at the same time. This does not detract from his omnipotence, but merely affirms that God cannot do the nonsensical. C. S. Lewis sums it up well:

> [God's] Omnipotence means power to do all that is intrinsically possible, not to do the intrinsically impossible. You may attribute miracles to Him, but not nonsense. This is no limit to his power. If you choose to say 'God can give a creature free will and at the same time withhold free will from it', you have not succeeded in saying anything about God: meaningless combinations of words do not suddenly acquire meaning simply because we prefix to them the two other words 'God can'. It remains true that all things are possible with God: the intrinsic impossibilities are not things but nonentities. It is no more possible for God than for the weakest of His creatures to carry out both of two mutually exclusive alternatives; not because His power meets an obstacle, but because nonsense remains nonsense even when we talk it about God.[3]

A world with morally significant freedom, in which people only choose good, is a contradiction in terms and is therefore impossible.

Surely a loving God would not allow suffering?

Questions about suffering usually involve cross-examining God, as if he were the only one to blame. Yet the flip side of human freedom is that we are also responsible for our actions. Free choice allows a meaningful existence, but it also opens up the possibility of wrong choice, and a large proportion of suffering can be attributed to the wrong choices of other people. If a pedestrian is knocked down and killed by a driver who was on the phone or texting while driving, is it really right to apportion blame firstly to God? Or should the driver be the first to stand up and account for his unspeakably foolish choices? Is God ultimately to blame for the holocaust of World War 2? Or does the blame really lie with Hitler, his twisted political ideologies and his like-minded advisors? I am not saying that God is completely free from responsibility. Of course not. It would be too simplistic to say that people are always to blame and God is not. But the point here is that when we demand our freedom and rights, we do not always own the responsibility and consequences of that freedom. Sometimes we are too quick to shift all of the blame for human suffering onto God, when in reality we need to take responsibility for some of it. Sometimes people do indeed abuse their God-given freedom.

So how does this help us answer the question: 'Surely a loving God would not allow people to suffer?' Many conclude that because we live in a world of suffering, God must not be loving. However, I would like to suggest that it is precisely *because* God is loving that we also have to live amongst suffering. Because God is loving, he has given humankind the dignity of freedom, but it is through the misuse of that freedom that much human suffering is brought about. God does not necessarily cause the suffering: he allows circumstances out of which suffering might be a possibility. But people have made it a reality.

Freedom to choose or reject God

This freedom has implications not just for how we live, but who we follow. Richard Dawkins begins his book *The God Delusion* by addressing people who have been raised in a religious home, secretly wanting out but never feeling like they could leave their religion. The very opening of the book reads,

As a child, my wife hated her school and wished she could leave. Years later, when she was in her twenties, she disclosed this unhappy fact to her parents, and her mother was aghast: 'But darling, why didn't you come to us and tell us?' Lalla's reply is my text for today: 'But I didn't know I could.'

I didn't know I could.

I suspect – well, I am sure – that there are lots of people out there who have been brought up in some religion or other, are unhappy in it, don't believe it, or are worried about the evils that are done in its name; people who feel vague yearnings to leave their parents' religion and wish they could, but just don't realize that leaving is an option. If you are one of them, this book is for you.[4]

Whatever your religion, whatever your background, whether you feel duty-bound or not, the Christian God has given you real freedom. Why? Because he loves us. He has done this in full knowledge of the cost involved, that humans may use their freedom to follow or reject him. Jesus encountered many people during his time and offered them a new start. Some chose to accept, but many also walked away and he let them do so. Lalla didn't know she had a choice in her schooling. But God intends that people always choose whether or not they follow him. There are life-changing reasons why you might want to choose God, but nevertheless you are free to walk towards him or to walk away.

Does God ever intervene?

Even if God has given people free choice, surely that does not excuse him completely? Surely he could still intervene to stop truly horrendous evils? This is both a valid question and a very difficult one to answer because it relies on the absence of evidence for proof. Moreover, what would intervention from God look like? Must it be dramatic or more subtle? It is certainly possible that God has intervened and stopped evils that we know nothing about. For example, why is it that, although we are capable of destroying our planet, we have not yet succeeded in doing so? Some great evils may well have been averted at crisis point, thanks to the hard work and diplomacy of those involved. We cannot rule out the possibility that a transcendent God has intervened on matters far bigger than our horizons, without people knowing anything about it.

Another way in which God may intervene extraordinarily is when people ask him for help. Many people have stories to tell of restored sound sleep after years of insomnia; of tumours shrinking or disappearing; of estranged wives, husbands or children being reconciled, despite the deep rifts that forced them apart; of resolved conflict in the office; of deep depression lifting. These people would all say that the reason the odds were defied was because God intervened. But how can this be so if God doesn't meddle with free choice? He does it precisely by cooperating with our freely made decision to ask him for help. This is what Christians call prayer. There are many different forms of prayer and meditation out there, but a Christian believes that the God they are asking help from firstly *wants* to help because he is completely good, and secondly is *able* to help because he is completely powerful. If we choose to ask this God for help, then he is free to intervene without interfering with our free will.

The mystery of evil

A wealthy man, well respected in his home town, encountered sudden disaster. He lost most of his possessions overnight when his business was raided and destroyed by fire and the workers stabbed. No sooner had he been told this, when the news came that all of his children had been killed when a building had collapsed on them. As if that were not enough to bear, he himself became severely ill with a debilitating skin disease that left him bereft of dignity and in agony. Some friends came to see him and were speechless for days because his suffering was too great for words. However, when they did open their mouths, cold comfort came out. They each tried to give reasons why their friend had suffered much, but no answers were satisfactory, and they would have been better off staying silent.

At the beginning of this chapter I suggested that a benevolent, omnipotent God permits evil because he has sufficient reasons for doing so. However, it would be easy to assume that, if God has good reasons, then people would know them and agree with them. But this does not necessarily follow. Just because we don't comprehend God's reasons for permitting evil doesn't mean there aren't any. The philosopher Stephen Wykstra likens this to the search for a dog compared with the search for a flea in a garage. If we look in our garage for a dog but don't see one, it is reasonable to conclude that the dog is not there. But looking for a flea and not finding one does not permit the same conclusion, since fleas are harder to find than dogs.[5] It may well be that the reasons of an infinite God are inaccessible to finite minds, more like 'fleas' than 'dogs'. God may permit evil for reasons beyond our capacity to understand.

The once-wealthy man in the story above lived 3,800–4,000 years ago. His name was Job, and his story is one of the earliest accounts in the Bible. The conversation between Job and his unhelpful friends went on and on, and Job became increasingly frustrated. God was strangely silent throughout their discourse, until the very end when he finally spoke to Job in such a way that silenced everyone:

> Who is this that questions my wisdom
>   with such ignorant words?
> Brace yourself like a man,
>   because I have some questions for you,
>   and you must answer them.
> (Job 38:2–3 NLT)

God then proceeded to ask Job fifty-two questions one after the other, including:

Where were you when I laid the foundations of the earth?
    Tell me, if you know so much.
(Job 38:4 NLT)

Have you ever commanded the morning to appear
    and caused the dawn to rise in the east?
 (Job 38:12 NLT)

Where does light come from,
    and where does darkness go?
Can you take each to its home?
    Do you know how to get there?
But of course you know all this!
For you were born before it was all created,
    and you are so very experienced!
(Job 38:19–21 NLT)

Will you discredit my justice
    and condemn me just to prove you are right?
Are you as strong as God?
    Can you thunder with a voice like his?
(Job 40:8–9 NLT)

Finally Job replies to God,

I know that you can do anything,
    and no one can stop you.
You asked, 'Who is this that questions my wisdom with such
        ignorance?'
    It is I – and I was talking about things I knew nothing about,
    things far too wonderful for me.
 (Job 42:2–3 NLT)

In attempting to answer the question: 'Why doesn't God stop
evil before it happens?', I will end as I began. There is a level at

which we are speaking about things too mysterious to understand fully. Why are some children abused, but others rescued just in time? Why do some terror plots succeed, but others are diverted? Why do some lorries have head-on collisions, but others swerve and avoid a crash? There are no easy answers. But the God to whom we ask the questions is one so powerful that the questions he has for us will silence us far more quickly than the questions we have for him.

What kind of freedom?

Many people would concur that a world with real freedom is the most preferable type, but at the same time the question: 'Why doesn't God stop evil?' asks that there be limits imposed upon human freedom. There is an inconsistency here. Do we want unlimited freedom or do we want God to intervene? The Christian view is that we need both, but that it is the very intervention of God in an individual's life that leads to real freedom. We will discuss this paradox further in subsequent chapters.

Do we want unlimited freedom or do we want God to intervene?

It is also crucial to say that this is not the end of the story. God does not always intervene to stop evil at present. One day he intends to remove it altogether, but for now he is allowing good and evil to exist alongside each other for a time. In chapter 8: 'Can a broken story be fixed?' I will explore this some more. God will completely remove evil precisely because he has ultimate power over it and over the course of human history. It is on the basis of God's intention to remove evil that Christians, including Will, can speak of having comfort in the present and also hope for the future.

4 Surely religion is the cause of so much suffering?

Most people can remember what they were doing on 11 September 2001. The impact of that day has left a lasting impression on us all. The cause? Religious convictions leading to violence and the suffering of many. Since 'September 11th' thousands of soldiers have given their lives in Afghanistan and Iraq in a war supposedly between the Islamic East and the Christian West, many of whom neither know nor care what they themselves believe. The *Times* columnist Melanie Reid voices a common frustration on the religious wars of the last decade:

> For years now I've felt this same visceral anger when young soldiers have died in wars where religion is the excuse for the conflict. Raw teenagers who joined up because they couldn't find work at home, or sought adventure beyond their Playstations; kids who had as little concept of God as they did of Godot, who lost and are still losing their lives in the dust of Afghanistan – purely because fanatics decided to blow them to bits in the name of extremist faith.[1]

No wonder this has led to the assertion that religion is the cause of so much suffering in our world. Who needs religion if this is what it leads to?

In Europe it did not begin with September 11th. Three thousand people have been killed in bombings or shootings across twenty-five years of terrorism in Northern Ireland, supposedly caused by tension between Protestants and Catholics. During the Crusades hundreds of thousands died as a result of holy war waged between Christians and Muslims. During the Reformation Christians burned each other at the stake, based on whether or not their allegiance was towards Rome. The Hindu caste system has condemned around 16% of its own population to a life of poverty because they are the lowest of the low: Dalits or 'untouchables'. Sharia law curbs women's rights and dignity in the Islamic world, and the news carries daily reports of the destruction and death caused by suicide bombings by Islamic extremists. In Britain we know all too well how this has now landed on our own doorstep with the 7 July 2005 attacks.

And what about the numerous reports of the sexual and physical abuse of children at the hands of priests? What about the stories of vicars who preach morality from the pulpit and yet are having an affair or dipping their hands into the collection plate? What about the people who call themselves Christians and yet ignore you, both in and outside of church, because you are not *one of them*? We cannot blame people for saying things like: 'Religion causes more harm than good.' People are put off spiritual things because of the general feeling that religion has caused more suffering than anything else. The eighteenth-century satirist and writer Jonathan Swift summarized the sentiment well: 'We have just enough religion to make us hate, but not enough to make us love one another.' Atheists today have put it more virulently. Richard Dawkins described religion as 'evil',[2] and the late Christopher Hitchens claimed that 'religion poisons everything'.[3]

What is religion?

The term 'religion' evokes a variety of different emotions and is defined in differing ways. For some it symbolizes stuffy institutions led by the emotionally truncated. For others it is a list of unattainable dos and don'ts. For others, it is a reminder of a childhood obligation that we have long since outgrown. But what actually is religion? As Keith Ward points out in his book, *Is Religion Dangerous?*,[4] scholars have found it difficult to arrive at a truly objective, unbiased definition. The *Oxford English Dictionary* defines it in several ways. The first definition reads: 'The belief in and worship of a superhuman controlling power, especially a personal God or gods'. Though God or gods are included, the definition does not refer exclusively to them. Other examples of superhuman controlling powers could be powerful aliens from outer space, superheroes such as Batman and Superman, the occult and, come to mention it, the 'mind genes' or memes that Richard Dawkins proposes influence our thought patterns and beliefs.[5] So it would seem that this definition of religion encompasses not only the major world faiths such as Judaism, Christianity, Islam, Buddhism and Hinduism, but also certain forms of atheism.

The second definition is: 'A particular system of faith and worship'. But what is faith? Many misunderstand faith, seeing it as a blind leap into the unknown. I would argue the opposite. Faith is something or someone you are building your life around because you are convinced of the evidence for its truthfulness. Christianity speaks of faith in a person, Jesus Christ, who really existed and who shed light, not darkness, on the human condition. That said, faith still reaches a point where the belief is persuasive but cannot be conclusively proven. People are quick to apply this to Christianity, but, as the theologian Alister McGrath points out in his book *Dawkins' God*,[6] the same is true of atheism. It is impossible to prove beyond doubt either that God does or does not exist. On this basis, atheism is as much a

faith as Christianity. The 'new atheist' evangelists who passion-
ately and aggressively espouse that 'religion is dangerous' are
living out their faith, their positive and liberating belief that God
does not exist, and the necessity of awakening others to this fact.
Well aware of the implications, Dawkins' position is that God is
'unlikely' rather than 'conclusively disproven',[7] as reflected in the
Atheist Bus Campaign adverts of 2009: 'There's *probably* no God.
Now stop worrying and enjoy your life.'

The final definition reads: 'A pursuit or interest followed with
great devotion'. Such a broad definition could include many
things. People are fiercely devoted followers of football, purchas-
ing season tickets and hardly daring to miss a game, at times
being willing to commit violence
to defend the honour of their
team. Consumerism is a national
interest, and such is our devotion
that we are willing to leave our
warm beds to queue in the early
hours of a midwinter morning
for the Boxing Day sales. The lives
of the rich and famous are closely
monitored through *OK!* and *Hello!* magazines. Watching soap
operas, reality TV, home renovation programmes and the
everyday person living their dream on TV is a pursuit that many
devote hours and hours to every week. Even the 'self' has openly
become an object of great devotion.[8] Put in these terms, many
things come under the category of 'religion', extending far
beyond the traditional world faiths. It is not that some people are
religious devotees and others are not. No, we are *all* devoted to
something. But we choose to devote ourselves to different things.

We are all devoted to something. But we choose to devote ourselves to different things.

If we allow religion to be defined in these terms, then we can
make a strong case that pursuing anything with great devotion
could lead to suffering. The misery caused by wanting possessions that are out of reach, and getting into debt in order to have
them, is substantial. Football-related violence, for example in

Columbia where at least two leading players and one referee have been killed as a result of their disappointing performance, cannot be ignored.[9] The impact on children of absent parents who are devoted to their work is another example. When people accuse religion of causing suffering, it is important to clarify what we mean by this incredibly broad term.

But what about religion, science and politics?[10]

That said, most people have the traditional world faiths in mind when they ask this question, and the only satisfactory response is to agree. Yes, in some cases Christians, Muslims, Hindus and Buddhists have indeed caused a great deal of suffering, both historically and in the present day, and this chapter will make no attempt to defend religion.

However, it is worth asking why we attribute the cause of suffering to religion but not to other categories. The hydrogen bombs dropped on Hiroshima and Nagasaki killed hundreds of thousands and left an even greater number with defects, burns and radiation sickness. The Chernobyl nuclear disaster directly killed thirty-one, but the number of related premature cancer deaths could be many thousands.[11] The threat of nuclear warfare continues to create tension between Iran and Israel, and the Cuban missile crisis had East and West on the brink of a war that could have annihilated millions. And yet we never hear the objection that science is the cause of so much suffering. Why not?

Equally, politics has been responsible for the suffering of many. Nazism in Germany and communism in Russia, spilling over into the Eastern bloc and China, have overshadowed torture and executions, not to mention brutal labour camps and the tearing apart of families. Eleven to fourteen million people, including up to 6 million Jews, died in Hitler's holocaust, not to mention the countless others who lost their lives fighting. At least 3 million and possibly up to 20 million died under Stalin; as many as

50 million may have died in Mao's China; and up to 2 million under Pol Pot in Cambodia's 'killing fields', especially if deaths from starvation, as well as brutality, are included. In South America, thousands have 'disappeared' in connection with right-wing political campaigns. And yet we never hear the objection that politics is the cause of so much suffering. Why not?

One possibility is because there is an assumption that science and politics are perceived as morally neutral, whereas religion is not. Science and politics could be used for good or bad, depending on whose hands they are in, but religion is not morally neutral. It is always supposed to offer a better way of living. Perhaps the question is asked of religion because buried deep within the question is the hope that religion *ought not* to be the cause of any suffering. Religion is supposed to be good, which is why the religious who stumble make such great head-lines. It is unexpected, surprising and disappointing that religion is the cause of so much suffering.

Would removing God solve the problem?

As we look back through history and trace patterns of suffering, we don't primarily learn about religion or politics or science. We learn about people. People are cruel to one another. Yes, suffering may occur within a particular political or religious regime, but the decision to apply the electrodes or curb rights or withhold food or bring down the machete is a decision of the human heart to ignore conscience, listen to fear and give way to evil.

But who decides how people treat one another? One of the beliefs that galvanized the twentieth century was that in nineteenth-century Europe it became acceptable to reject belief in God. Stifling, institutionalized Christianity had given way to loud and eloquent voices declaring that God was no longer a viable option and humanity was his replacement. In Britain, as Alister McGrath points out, the poet A. C. Swinburne reworked the Christian hymn, 'We Praise You, O God' into 'We Praise You, O Man', and wrote in his 'Hymn of Man':

> Thou art smitten, thou God, thou art smitten; thy death is upon
> thee, O Lord.
> And the love-song of earth as thou diest resounds through the
> wind of her wings –
> Glory to Man in the highest! for Man is the master of things.[12]

In Germany the philosopher Friedrich Nietzsche, at the gateway to the twentieth century, announced with force and finality that God was dead, his coffin had been sealed and at his funeral humankind, the *Übermensch* or Superman, will take charge. He himself predicted that as a result the years ahead would be bleak and violent. He was right. When the human race is the decider of how people treat one another, things become very grim indeed. McGrath put it like this:

> If any worldview is rendered incredible by the suffering and pain
> of the twentieth century, it is the petty dogma of the nineteenth
> century, which declared that humanity was divine. It requires an
> act of blind faith to ignore the moral wasteland of the twentieth
> century to agree with the shallow judgement of Algernon
> Charles Swinburne (1837–1909): 'Glory to man in the highest! /
> For man is the master of things.' This 'master of things' has much
> to answer for – more violence, bloodshed, and oppression than
> any naïve Victorian optimist could ever have imagined.
>   Nearly two hundred years' experience of the moral failings
> of this humanity-turned-divinity have been enough to convince
> most that it has been a failed experiment. While some continue
> to argue that Auschwitz disproves the existence of God, many
> more would argue that it demonstrates the depths to which
> humanity, unrestrained by any thought or fear of God, will sink.
> There are many today who affirm a belief in humanity in
> preference to a belief in God. Yet this humanity has been

responsible for a series of moral, social, and political catastrophes, some inspired by a belief in God, others by a belief that God must be eliminated, by all means and at all costs. The common denominator here is humanity, not divinity.[13]

If the rules for living are decided from within the human race, then the events of the twentieth century are exactly what we should expect. If the lid has been lifted on right and wrong, then all sorts of atrocities, though abhorrent to the majority, not only become possible, they become permissible. In contrast, if the Christian God, a God who is perfectly pure and holy, who commands us not to murder (Matthew 5:21)[14] and to love not only our friends but also our enemies (Matthew 5:44–48),[15] decides how people treat one another, then atrocities committed by Christians defy these commands. Just because something terrible is done in the name of Christianity does not mean it has been done in the spirit of Christianity. Indeed atrocities committed in the name of Christianity are fundamentally at odds with the message of Christianity.

Jesus was anti-religion

During the year I spent at theological college one of my friends decided to set up a table in a busy shopping street, with the aim of providing a place to deal with people's questions about Christianity. The table had a banner attached to it containing the words 'Imagine No Religion' from the John Lennon song. Numerous people came up to my friend, thinking they were approaching an atheist. They were of course very surprised to discover that he was a Christian. This was a reminder to my friend that many think that being a Christian is about being religious, largely because Jesus himself was a good religious teacher, perhaps the most religious person ever to have lived. But this does raise an interesting question: Why then did the religious authorities hate him so much? And why did they eventually have him killed? If Jesus was so religious, he would have rubbed shoulders much more with the religious crowd, but he didn't. In fact, some of Jesus' harshest words were reserved for the religious of his day (Matthew 22 – 24).[16] Why? Was he just doing it for 'show'? Was he leading a rebellion? Did he take pleasure in finding fault? Or was there a much bigger point?

The original commandments of God to the Israelites were to 'love the LORD your God with all your heart and with all your soul and with all your strength' (Deuteronomy 6:5) and 'love your neighbour as yourself' (Leviticus 19:18), which included protecting the weakest in society, such as widows and orphans, and upholding justice. In other words, if God is made the priority in the human heart, then from that comes the capacity to love people of all shapes and sizes, weak and strong, rich and poor. And society works. When Jesus stepped into human history the spiritual scene was quite different. Some of the religious leaders had moved God to the sidelines, were putting self first and had invented hundreds of extra laws and spiritual hoops for the people to jump through in order to be on good terms with God. The weak and vulnerable were neglected, and people, as in many religious communities today, were far from able to love their enemies; in fact they were more inclined to hate their neighbours.

Jesus declared himself anti-religious. He described God, his Father, not as someone who makes people jump through religious hoops in order to earn religious brownie points, but as a person who searches for and pursues people in order for them to return to him. Why? Because God is love, not religion. Not rules, but relationship. He reminded the religious experts at one point that their 'neighbour' was the people-group living down the road whom they had hated since birth: the Samaritans (Luke 10:25–37). He set impossible standards for living, instructing people to 'be perfect' at one point, 'as your heavenly Father is perfect' (Matthew 5:48). Is such a standard even possible? Yes,

Jesus would say, but only by abandoning religion, because God is not a rule to be obeyed, as religion would have it, but a person whom you can know. A person who is capable of transforming the human heart so that extra-ordinary love can be extended to people we might otherwise hate, so that widows can be protected, so that the lowest of the low, the 'untouchables' in society, can be given dignity, honour and the same opportunities as everyone else. Alister and Joanna McGrath put it like this:

God is love, not religion. Not rules, but relationship.

> Jesus of Nazareth did no violence to anyone. He was the object, not the agent, of violence. Instead of meeting violence with violence, rage with rage, Christians are asked to 'turn the other cheek', and 'not to let the sun go down on their anger'. This is about the elimination of the roots of violence – no, more than that: it is about its transfiguration.[17]

The desire that religion ought not to be the cause of any suffering is good and right. It should not be ignored or cynically cast aside. That desire exists because it is possible to satisfy it, but not in any and every religion. In fact, not in religion at all. It is satisfied through the person of Jesus, who set impossible standards for living and then himself gave us the capacity to live them by changing the human heart.

Is religion the cause of so much suffering? I am inclined to agree with the questioner and say 'yes', because religion, in its traditional understanding, is a phenomenon of human origin in which people use rituals to climb their way to God. Religion is what happens when people want to be spiritual, but insist on relying on their own wisdom and resources and religious laws to get there. Religious laws, including those in the Bible, highlight above all humanity's inability to keep them! History has shown that people are unable to 'be perfect' without external help, and therefore the outworking of religion could be anything from an unfriendly face in church to the slaughter of innocents who do not share our views. Jesus' message in first-century Palestine was to live a life which says, shouts even, 'Imagine no religion!' Have you ever wondered what a world without religion would look like? Imagine not having to try to climb the ladder yourself, but instead imagine that God climbed down the ladder to us and did for us what we could not do for ourselves. It might seem the last place worth looking, but take a good long look at Jesus.

But aren't Christians hypocrites?

Why then, if God is capable of changing the human heart, do Christians not always live up to his standards? So many people turn their back on God because of the messed-up Christians they have met who seem to behave more like the religious authorities of Jesus' day than Jesus himself. As Mahatma Gandhi once commented, 'I like your Christ; I do not like your Christians. Your Christians are so unlike your Christ.' The accusation that 'Christians are hypocrites' is common and indeed sometimes warranted.[18]

The only correct response is to recognize that hypocrisy is real, that Christians do not always get it right and thereby have caused others to reject Christ. Sometimes this happens where people are operating under the name of Christianity but following rules rather than Christ. At other times people are genuine followers of Christ, experiencing struggles on their journey. Yes, Jesus changes people for the better, and this is both instantaneous and a lifelong process with successes and failures along the way, because God will not change us beyond what we are willing to allow. Once again God, the respecter of human choice, does not force our hand but cooperates with our will. If there are areas of life that we keep locked away, then this may lead to behaviour that does not match up to Christ's.

That said, the fact that Christians do not always get it right is also exactly the point. Being a Christian is not about being a holier-than-thou person who has it all together. It is about being forgiven by God for failing to live up to our own standards, let alone any others. It is about recognizing that we can't do it on our own and need help. This is why Jesus said, 'It is not the healthy who need a doctor, but the sick. I have not come to call the righteous, but sinners' (Mark 2:17 NIV 1984). In other words, I have not come for those who think they are doing fine but for those who realize they are not. Right at the core of Christianity is a recognition of weakness. Therefore it is not surprising that the weaknesses of its adherents might be visible at times.

Has Christianity done any good at all?

A few years ago my husband and I were having dinner with Italian friends and discussing, as you do over dinner, the condition of European society. That is, is it declining, improving or in status quo? One of our friends commented that he thought that Europe was definitely at a high point in terms of quality of life. Admittedly our conversation took place before the financial crisis, and his response might well be different today. And yet, despite current-day austerity measures, there is a general opinion that, though Christianity is at a low point in Europe, we are the most civilized, most developed, most liberated that we have ever been. Technological advances have enabled travel and communication across the globe; medical advances have increased adult lifespan and decreased child mortality; social advances have closed the gap between rich and poor.

Many vocal atheists today conclude that the decline of Christianity has freed up European society. Yet others argue that the opposite is true. Our Judeo-Christian foundations have formed the backbone of Western society and have undergirded Western approaches to art, education, music, science, medicine, reason, history, justice, democracy and human rights. Keith Ward puts it like this:

> Christians have founded hospitals, hospices, schools and universities. They have sponsored great works of painting, sculpture, literature and music. Giotto, Rembrandt, Michelangelo, Dante, Augustine, Milton, Palestrina, J.S. Bach, Mozart – without their religiously inspired creative vision the world would be poorer. It was in Christian Europe that investigation into the world as the creation of one wise, rational God gave rise to modern science. Copernicus (a lay canon of the church), Kepler, Francis Bacon, Isaac Newton – all were inspired to investigate the natural world because of their belief that it was wisely ordered and accessible to human reason, the image of the reason of the creator . . . The eighteenth-century Enlightenment itself, with its call for faith in human reason and its concern for human flourishing and happiness, can plausibly be seen as a recovery of primal Christian belief in the rationality of the world, the unique dignity of human life, and an insistence on the vocation of every individual to realize their God-given potentialities. It was in this context that the critical study of history arose, as Christians began to examine the origins of their faith in a series of particular historical events. And it was in this context that belief in full freedom of conscience and equality before God, and in universal human rights and the ideal of universal participation in government, developed from basic belief in human personhood as created in the image of God – free, rational and responsible . . . It would be absurd to say that Christianity was the only cause of these things . . . But it would be even more nonsensical to deny the major role that the Christian religion has played in the formation of Europe and its rich cultural heritage.[19]

Only Christianity made a difference

Precisely because of the power of Jesus Christ to change the human heart, there have been many situations worldwide in which Christianity has made a remarkable difference, often when all other methods have failed. Situations in which the Christians involved are living or have lived true to Christ. Let's look at a selection from around the world.

Hong Kong

The missionary Jackie Pullinger MBE has seen over 1,000 opium addicts set free from their addictions over the last five decades in Hong Kong. Many addicts did not encounter withdrawal symptoms, which Christians have attributed to their being prayed for round the clock. Many of the triad gangs in the Walled City have been disbanded, and the cycle of violent revenge broken, to the extent that Jackie's work has been recognized by the Hong Kong and British governments. Her compelling story can be found in the book *Chasing the Dragon*.[20]

Ecuador

In the 1950s five missionaries gave their lives in the cause of contacting and transforming one of the most violent tribes in the world. At that time over 60% of deaths within the Auca tribe were due to homicide revenge killings, such that the tribe itself was on the verge of extinction. Jim Elliot, Nate Saint, Ed McCully, Peter Flemming and Roger Youderian were speared to death in their twenties by men who knew no other way when afraid than to kill. *LIFE* magazine and others reported it, questioning the wisdom of these men who could have had promising careers back in the USA. Yet the wives of the dead men remained in Ecuador to see most of the tribe turn to Christ, including those who had killed their husbands. Some of their children grew up with the Aucas, including Nate's son, Pete. Such was the trans-formation and depth of friendship with the tribe that Pete Saint's son gave the name 'grandfather' to the man who had killed his biological grandfather. The homicide rate in the tribe has now fallen by 90%.

South Africa

The Truth and Reconciliation Commission (TRC) had a key role in rebuilding South Africa at the end of apartheid. After Nelson Mandela's election racial tension was high, voices on both sides were silent, and the government needed to find a way to deal with the past and move towards a unified society. One of the key tenets of the TRC was openly to consider amnesty to those who were willing to confess the atrocities they had participated in, whether they opposed or supported apartheid. Archbishop Desmond Tutu, on his appointment as Chairman of the TRC, said,

> I hope that the work of the commission, by opening wounds to cleanse them, will thereby stop them from festering . . . True reconciliation is never cheap, for it is based on forgiveness, which is costly. Forgiveness in turn depends on repentance, which has to be based on an acknowledgement of what was done wrong, and therefore on disclosure of the truth. You cannot forgive what you do not know.[21]

The South African government also recognized that 'to err is human but to forgive is divine'. Despite some imperfections, the TRC was regarded as crucial in the transition to democracy, and Desmond Tutu received the Nobel Peace Prize for his work in 1987.

Northern Ireland

A final example comes from the town of Enniskillen in Northern Ireland. On 8 November 1987 the IRA set off a bomb during a Remembrance Day parade, killing eleven people and injuring sixty-three others. Student nurse Marie Wilson was attending the parade with her father Gordon. Both were buried under the rubble, and Gordon held Marie's hand until they were both pulled out. Marie had lost consciousness and she died later that day in hospital. People from Enniskillen and beyond were left devastated and outraged.

A few hours after the bombing Gordon Wilson was interviewed by the BBC. He said publicly that he bore 'no grudge'[22] against those who had killed his daughter. He said that he would pray for them and also asked that no-one take revenge for his daughter's death, because it would not bring her back and he wanted the peaceful relations between Catholics and Protestants in Enniskillen to continue. Mr Wilson's radical approach had a major impact both nationally and internationally, and succeeded in promoting peace and preventing acts of vengeance in the aftermath of the bombing. He dedicated the rest of his life to working for reconciliation between people in Northern Ireland. The Irish government in Dublin rewarded his work by making him a senator in the Irish parliament.

No religion could have caused Gordon Wilson to seek forgiveness instead of revenge, and peace instead of retaliation. Only a major work of God in the human heart can lead a person to forgive callous violence amid their own raw grief mere hours after losing a cherished daughter. If Gordon Wilson had sought revenge, then 'religion' would surely have been the cause of even more suffering, as has indeed been the case in Northern Ireland. Instead he allowed the God who is able to break destructive cycles of revenge to do his work. The work of an invisible God had visible and lasting effects in Northern Ireland.

Matthew Parris, the English journalist and atheist, lived in Malawi as a boy and revisited it as an adult to see the work of a British charity. In an article in *The Times*, he wrote that the work of this charity

renew[ed] my flagging faith in development charities. But travelling in Malawi refreshed another belief, too: one I've been trying to banish all my life, but an observation I've been unable to avoid since my African childhood. It confounds my ideological beliefs, stubbornly refuses to fit my worldview, and has embarrassed my growing belief that there is no God.

Now a confirmed atheist, I've become convinced of the enormous contribution that Christian evangelism makes in Africa: sharply distinct from the work of secular NGOs, government projects and international aid efforts. These alone will not do. Education and training alone will not do. In Africa Christianity changes people's hearts. It brings a spiritual transformation. The rebirth is real. The change is good.[23]

Grace's story

I was raised in a loving and encouraging home. My parents are church leaders, and for as long as I can remember I was brought to church and told stories about God and who he is. I began to speak at an early age, and at seventeen months old could quote all of John 3:16 (NKJV): 'For God so loved the world that He gave His only begotten Son, that whoever believes in Him should not perish but have everlasting life.' My parents encouraged me not only in the Christian faith, but also in other ways, as I was intelligent and talented. I had a real passion for singing and from the age of four or five was already performing publicly.

My mum was a PE teacher and very much into physical fitness and encouraging other young people to stay in shape. Since we didn't have much money at the time, a close family friend used to make a lot of our clothes. This friend made an off-hand comment to my mum: 'You should probably watch your daughter because her measurements are a bit bigger than those of other children.' It wasn't a significant comment, but because my mum was into personal fitness she started encouraging me to do more exercise, so I joined lots of sports teams: football, volleyball and so on. From the age of five or six I was put on diets, and at primary school my mum would come in and bring me a different lunch from everybody else's so that I wouldn't become overweight. She wasn't making undue fuss, just trying to be responsible.

I don't think this affected me at first, but from about seven or eight I started to lack confidence about the way I looked. I began to think, 'Given that I am fat, what can I do to be acceptable? What else can I find my worth in?' I had the idea, maybe sub-consciously, that if I couldn't be perfect in body, then I was going to be perfect in performance, both academically and vocally. I started to really excel at school and wasn't happy unless I got the highest mark. I also began to sing for all I was worth: in opening ceremonies, choirs, church services, solo performances, voice competitions, and in addition I was having voice training.

Towards the end of high school I looked into securing music scholarships at prestigious universities. An audition came up, and I was really excited. I had to perform a few pieces, but midway through a performance the panel stopped me and asked, 'Do you find that you are losing your voice a lot? Do you sometimes taste blood? Do you find that the notes don't last as long as they should?' I had never told anyone about this and wondered how on earth they knew. My audition was over. I was strongly urged to see a specialist and handed a phone number. I was told that I was in danger not only of losing my singing voice, but also my speaking voice because from such a young age I had overused my vocal cords.

My world shattered because, without being conscious of it at the time, I had placed so much value on my ability to perform. I began a long journey of treatment. I was diagnosed with polyps or nodules on my vocal cords, and at the age of fifteen had surgery to remove them, with the likelihood that I would not be able to sing again in the same way. Everything I had planned, everything that my self-worth was invested in, seemed to be going out of the window.

The surgery went well, but as part of my recovery I needed vocal therapy to learn how to speak and sing again. Over the course of the next year I went for therapy up to twice a week. I needed to miss a lot of school for this, and so my grades started to fall, and with them the only remaining thing that gave my life meaning. I started to feel like I was trapped, in darkness really. Everything I thought I was confident in had been stripped away. When I looked at myself, I realized that I hated myself. I hated who I was; I hated my body; I hated this image that people had accepted because it was based only on how I could perform.

The only way in which I knew to respond was to change myself physically. If I couldn't perform, then I had to make myself beautiful, more presentable. In my earlier dieting, people had tended to congratulate me when I lost weight, so I started on a journey of not eating. It wasn't very intense at first, but one thing led to another. Eventually I was going with very long stretches of not eating, or else bingeing and then purging. I found diet pills and sometimes took huge quantities of them, using whatever means I could find to control my appearance. Unfortunately, people didn't realize what was going on. They were encouraging and congratulated me on having lost weight. But all that did was serve to feed the destructive cycle.

So I started to go on a deeper downward spiral of not eating at all. Even people's approval of the weight-loss stopped, and then I was in a much deeper and darker hole. The images I knew people had of me on the outside, this performing little girl with a beautiful voice, were fake on the inside. I was face to face with who I was and I was disgusted, so I started to take the hurt from the inside and make it a reality on the outside. When I was frustrated or alone or feeling sad, I would hurt myself physically, but no-one really knew.

I remember sitting alone one day in my room after one of the more violent self-harming incidences, staring up at the ceiling and screaming, 'Oh God, if you are actually there, where are you? God, if you actually love me, why, why has this happened?

Why do I feel like this? Why aren't you real? If you are out there, then make yourself known to me, because I don't think it's real! It's a load of rubbish, and nobody knows the darkness that's inside of me. Everyone still thinks I'm a shiny, happy person.'

I wouldn't say that at that moment anything really changed. Throughout school I continued to battle this idea that I was fake and that the God I had been taught about all my life wasn't really there, helping and rescuing me. But towards the end of school I remember hearing a message on the Bible verse I mentioned earlier: 'For God so loved the world that He gave His only begotten Son, that whoever believes in Him should not perish but have everlasting life.' From that one verse, the speaker told the message of the cross, a message of suffering, a message that God loved the world and loved me so much that he had suffered the worst pain, the worst violence and the worst rejection of anyone. All for me. All because he loved me; that's why he went through it. I had heard that verse all my life; I had recited it at seventeen months, and yet the reality of the truth of the cross of Jesus crashed in on me in a way that it had never done before, heavier than any broken heart or lost expectations or hurt that had crashed in over the years. The intense suffering Jesus went through on my behalf meant that I was loved and accepted not for what I could do, not for how I looked, not for who I could impress, not for how many pounds I could shed, but just for who I was. All I could think and say at that point over and over and over again were the words, 'He loves me, oh my goodness, he loves me so much that he did this for me.'

So that really began my road out of the darkness, out of the struggle, out of the self-harming and eating disorders. I want to be honest and say that my battle with self-image did not have a quick fix. But the reality was that the God of the universe had actually come to me. When I had yelled at the ceiling my screams had been heard by a God who had already gone to great lengths to show me that I was of value and worth. I sought help and talked to people who were close to me, letting them into this secret dichotomized world I had created for myself. Every new day, sometimes every new hour, when I felt that urge to hate or prove myself or felt the darkness closing in, I reminded myself that Jesus had met me in my pain and that he loved me.

Sometimes I ask why this has happened, and there's never any great answer. But I do know that Christianity isn't just for that broken, dark place; I've grown from there and have all the more confidence to know that Jesus is real. Sometimes I have to look in the mirror and choose to see what God sees, believe what God sees. In times of stress or pressure I have to choose to keep my eating and exercising habits consistent, and it starts with daily, sometimes hourly, coming back to the truth that I'm loved, I'm cared for and I don't have to do this on my own. God has also surrounded me with people who know my story, people who can encourage me along the way and ask me the right questions. One of these people is the wonderful husband that God brought into my life. We also have a daughter and are raising her to know that she is loved and accepted by us, but even more so by her heavenly Father.

The difference today is that I'm whole. I'm not broken any more. Jesus Christ has made me whole. I know who I am because I know who he is.

5 If God exists, then does he care about my suffering?

When Conrad is in a period of illness he spends a lot of time alone. Visitors are a wonderful source of company and re-connection to the outside world. Over the years many dear friends and family have sat with Conrad, eaten dinner with him, read to him, prayed with him, told him jokes, cried with him, all at a cost to their own time and energy. A compassionate and well-timed visitor lifts the spirits and deepens friendships.

In contrast, I find it harder to be around other people. All the questions about how Conrad is doing are directed to me. During Conrad's last illness our children were two and four years old respectively, and I was already fielding their three questions a minute, so how could I find the energy to answer yet more questions? Besides, I did not have the answers and over time came to dread being asked.

I noticed the different ways in which well-meaning people act towards a person in pain. Some did not ask questions at all. Some offered very welcome practical help, such as meals and childcare that kept our family afloat. Some felt awkward and skirted around the subject and talked about everything *but*

Conrad. Some were happy to talk about Conrad, but forgot to ask the one question I *was* able to answer: How was *I* doing? Some offered their own ill-informed diagnoses of the problem: It's caused by stress; it's chronic fatigue; it's psychological. Some offered the greeting-card message engraved on our culture of 'get well soon'. The problem was that it felt like my husband was going to 'stay sick long'! Some were keen to relay their own personal suffering and offer reassurance that they knew exactly how I was feeling. Sometimes this was true, but sometimes it wasn't. Sometimes the reactions of others only increased my sense of isolation.

And yet some people were a great source of comfort to us and knew just what to say and when to say it. Some knew when there was no need even to use words, and that a greater level of empathy was expressed through silence than through speech. Some of our greatest comforters seemed to be those who themselves had suffered in a similar way, or were still suffering, or had watched loved ones suffer. I was drawn to these people more than others. Why? Because I felt understood by them. There was something significant about our shared experiences of suffering. It was comforting to know that we were not alone in our suffering, and also encouraging to see that others had struggled like us and yet had found a way through.

If God were one of those people in the room, what would be his reaction to my suffering? Is he someone we would want to approach? Would he be socially awkward, wanting to skirt around the topic? Would he be sensitive and compassionate? Or would he bulldoze his way into the conversation? If he exists at all, is he someone who cares and understands, or would he add to my sense of isolation? If God exists, then how does he view my suffering?

Is God personal?

Perhaps surprisingly, the very asking of the question: 'Does God care?' represents a degree of failure in many of the world religions. The attribute of 'caring' goes hand in hand with personhood. Yet most religions do not speak of a personal God. For the atheist, the question points to a failure to live out the belief that matter is all there is; for the Muslim, failure to accept the will of Allah; for the Buddhist, failure to extinguish desire; for the Hindu, failure to transcend good and evil into the consciousness beyond.

This then raises a further question: If in the majority of the world religions God is not personal, then why is a personal God so frequently invoked? If the question: 'Does God care?' is secondary or void in most of the world religions, then why do so many of us ask it? Christianity is very often the last place people go to on their spiritual quest. Like launching a city-wide search-and-rescue operation for a missing child, but forgetting to check the house next door, many in the West view Christianity as the religion least likely to be relevant to their daily needs. Yet what does it have to say in response to whether or not God can be known personally?

Since before time began the Christian God has existed as one God in three persons: Father, Son and Holy Spirit. From the start of humankind people not only spoke to God, but also heard back from him. People conversed with God, argued with God, bartered with God, and some even persuaded God to change his mind on specific occasions. In first-century Palestine, God entered history as the person of Jesus. God was not just available for conversation, he was available as a whole living, breathing person. In Jesus, God is as personal as it is possible to be.

Now, in popular Western culture, people who speak to God and hear him speak back are generally viewed with suspicion. The possibility of hearing from God is something you must reach your own conclusions about, but if you adhere to different beliefs and yet have asked the question: 'Does God care?' or 'Why?' at some point in your life, to which God were you addressing the question? Does it matter to you? Did you have to embrace or suspend your original beliefs in order to ask that question?

Why is God doing this to me?

Just like the National Lottery used to depict a huge finger from the sky pinpointing certain individuals, many view their suffering as a personal punishment from God for something they have done or not done, or believed or not believed. Do some people suffer more than others because they somehow deserve it? Again, the different religions have different answers.

One answer is that this is just the way the world is. There is nothing you can do. Horoscopes, of which our magazines are full, tell us that the events of our lives are fixed and must simply be played out. And if they are not fixed in the stars, they are certainly fixed in our genes. You are your DNA. If you are ill, it is because a random genetic mutation has found its way into your family line. If you are attacked, it is because your attacker has a genetic predisposition towards extreme anger. If your spouse has left you for another person, it is because they have been driven by their biology or have followed their own feelings and preferences, which may or may not be the same as yours. Individuals are not singled out for suffering by some divine agent; suffering is simply part of life.

Another answer is that you are responsible for your predicament. In Eastern thought bad deeds from a previous life reap a punishment in this life, through the principle of *karma*. In Islam if you suffer, it could be to test your faith and obedience, or because sins from this life are receiving a come-uppance.

The Christian perspective does not absolve people of responsibility either. Sometimes suffering can result from foolish choices backfiring on us, for example overspending on the credit card and then struggling financially. However, the core of the Christian message is that suffering is not usually a personal punishment from God. It is a general consequence of living in a broken world, in which everyone is affected. Christians too get 'hit' by personal tragedy and suffering. Very often they didn't see it coming, have a strong sense of its cruelty and unfairness, and go through a whole range of very natural emotions in response.

Christians believe that the urge to ask the questions: 'Why me?' or 'Is this the way things are supposed to be?' or 'Does God care?' is within us because there is a dynamic Being to whom we are meant to address them. Personal questioning and wanting answers is not something to be quashed and ignored, but rather embraced. This Being is not someone who will crumble if we rant and rave at him, nor will he brush us off and remain aloof. He is a God whose biggest desire is that we turn to him and talk to him about whatever we are going through, and who has made it possible for us to do just that not only in religious places such as churches, but at any time and in any place. The question: 'Why . . . ?' occurs 510 times in the Bible. Its pages are packed with people being extremely real with God about their circumstances, expressing a range of human emotions, from the depths of despair and depression to elation, anger and beyond. Very often it is not pretty, but God listens and responds, and it seems that he comes close to those who are willing to be honest with him rather than shelter behind potted, politically correct prayers.

If you are to blame, should you be helped?

The streets of Oxford contain numerous homeless people, many of whom sell *The Big Issue* magazine to passers-by. I recall one occasion when I stopped to buy the magazine with a friend. As we walked on we discussed whether it was right or not to help a homeless person. As the conversation progressed it became apparent that my friend's view was that the homeless are to blame for their predicament and therefore should not be helped. They have clearly made poor choices and therefore deserve the situation they now find themselves in. The question of blame and punishment in suffering is a crucial matter for social justice. My friend's view was that, if people are to blame for their suffering, then they are simply getting what they deserve. But if they are not, then they should be helped out of their predicament.

Until 1947 the Hindu caste system shaped Indian society. It was based on the belief that everyone is reincarnated into a particular level of society, depending on the deeds of previous lives. Whereas some castes were of high status, such as the Brahminical caste, others such as Dalits (whom we met earlier), were at the bottom of the ladder. Even today the caste system still operates socially. Dalits can be denied education, excluded from Hindu society and restricted to the jobs considered impure by the higher castes, such as cleaning streets and sewers. The caste system survived for centuries because of the belief that the lower castes were reaping their punishment from previous lives and therefore did not merit help. Karma has its practical outworking.

That said, the recognition that people should help those less fortunate than themselves is put into practice by people of all religions, and there are organizations within all the world faiths working to alleviate suffering. However, the view that people are not necessarily to blame for their suffering is unique to Christianity, and has been the driving force behind countless movements aimed at relieving it. William Wilberforce campaigned along with others for much of his life to abolish the slave trade in 1807; Christian Aid was founded by British and Irish church leaders after World War II to help rebuild the lives of European refugees who had lost everything; Thomas Barnardo founded the charity Barnardo's in 1867 to help destitute children. Today Christians are among those raising awareness and campaigning for an end to sex trafficking (modern-day slavery) and global poverty. They can also be found helping people in desperate situations: in war zones, refugee camps, disease-infested hospitals, and so the list goes on.

If God is real and personal, then why doesn't he show himself?

People are fond of asking the question: 'If God is real and personal, then why doesn't he make himself more obvious to us? Why doesn't he make himself clearly visible if he wants people to believe in him?' The simple answer is, he did. But not in our lifetime, nor in our country, but 2,000 years ago in Roman-occupied Palestine. God who is outside of time stepped into time and space. He who was limitless allowed himself to become limited within the confines of a fragile baby's skin. The One who spoke life into existence allowed his speech to become restricted to a baby's lungs. The One who could move mountains allowed himself to be become dependent on people for his very survival. There is something shocking about this. The concept of God becoming a human being is absolutely absurd in any other religion; in fact believing it in some cultures could cost you your life. And yet if it is true, all sorts of things become possible.

The person being commended to you is Jesus Christ. Like all others, he was born as a baby and grew into a boy, and then a man. He encountered the same human experiences as us. Jesus knew what it felt like to be tired, rested, hungry, thirsty, sated, happy, sad, upset, angry, contented, appreciated, frustrated, misunderstood, loved and hated. Jesus experienced the pressure of work, often with little respite, as crowds of people tracked him down. He experienced acute grief when a close friend died, and his response outside his friend's tomb forms the shortest sentence in the New Testament: 'Jesus wept' (John 11:35). His relative, John the Baptist, was beheaded. His father, Joseph, may have died as Jesus was growing up. Jesus fully identified with life on earth by entering history, getting his hands dirty and experiencing life first-hand.

So why did God fully lower himself to human levels? Because he loves. God is love. Love is demonstrated by actions. We all know the saying: 'Actions speak louder than words.' If your partner tells you they love you but spends every weekend working or on Facebook, you might question whether their words were genuine. Words are backed up by actions. Actions qualify or disqualify words. God demonstrated his love for humanity by becoming one of us: 'This is how God showed his love among us: he sent his one and only Son into the world that we might live through him' (1 John 4:9).

> *So why did God fully lower himself to human levels? Because he loves. God is love.*

We object to Jesus' claims such as: 'I am the way and the truth and the life. No one comes to the Father except through me' (John 14:6). They are too exclusive. Who does he think he is? But look at what he is saying. He is saying that the Way, the Truth, is not a set of religious exercises, nor a set of philosophical statements, nor a marker that we must measure up to. No, the Truth is a person. The Truth has a face. In first-century Palestine you could smile at the Truth, eat dinner with the Truth, shout at the Truth, cry with the Truth, even kiss the Truth. God really became one of us. Our Christmases are dominated by Santa, socks, reindeer and red wine, and we have become anaesthetized to the magnitude of what God has done. He *has* made himself known. He *was* prepared to show himself. And the historical evidence documenting Jesus' existence surpasses that of any other historical figure of that era.[1] How much evidence do we need?

He bound up the broken

Often people can accept that God so loved *the world* that he gave his one and only Son, but many find it difficult to believe that God's love extends personally to them as individuals. Jesus spent a lot of time with individuals. He came to 'bind up the broken-hearted' (Isaiah 61:1), to restore sight to the blind and hearing to the deaf, to cause the lame to walk again, to cleanse sufferers of leprosy, to heal the sick, raise the dead and proclaim good news to the poor (Matthew 11:5; Luke 7:22). At the beginning of his public ministry Jesus said,

> The Spirit of the Lord is on me,
>   because he has anointed me
>   to proclaim good news to the poor.
> He has sent me to proclaim freedom for
>   the prisoners
>   and recovery of sight for the blind,
> to set the oppressed free.
> (Luke 4:18)

He sought out people in the crowd, including a woman who had been bleeding for twelve years. When she was healed by just touching his robe Jesus felt it and stopped to find her and speak to her (Luke 8:40–48). He gave her respect; her dignity was restored. When crowds of people came to him for healing, all went away restored, regardless of how long it took to do so. Individuals mattered to Jesus.

The suffering God

Jesus did not just observe suffering, but he endured it himself. He began 'to explain to his disciples that he must go to Jerusalem and suffer many things at the hands of the elders, the chief

priests and the teachers of the law, and that he must be killed
and on the third day be raised to life' (Matthew 16:21). They did
not understand at the time, but it happened.

In the last twenty-four hours of his life Jesus was subjected to
agonizing physical, emotional and psychological suffering. He
was betrayed into the hands of the authorities by a close friend,
disowned by another and deserted by the rest. Completely alone,
he was given an unfair, illegal trial, spat on, beaten up, flogged
within an inch of his life, and abused by a battalion of Roman
soldiers, before being led out to be crucified.

As he hung there passers-by mocked and shouted at Jesus, 'He
saved others . . . but he can't save himself! . . . Let him come
down now from the cross, and we will believe in him.' In other
words, 'If you are so powerful, God, why don't you stop this evil
from happening?' The same questions we ask of God today were
shouted in his face (Matthew 27:42). But even when exhausted,
humiliated and in agony on the cross, Jesus was still dealing with
the suffering around him. Two criminals were crucified on either
side of him. One hurled insults; the other asked, 'Jesus, remember
me when you come into your kingdom.' The reply? 'Truly I tell
you, today you will be with me in paradise' (Luke 23:42–43).
Individuals mattered. 'Remember me' was met with: 'You will
be with me.' Person to person.

The concept of the cross has become tamed in today's society.
The religious and irreligious alike wear crucifixes around their
necks as a piece of jewellery, but this would be akin to wearing
a gallows, an electric chair or a guillotine today. In Roman society
crucifixion was a brutal and degrading method of execution
reserved for the lowest of the low. Invented by the 'barbarians'
and later adopted by both Greeks and Romans, it was, in the
words of the late theologian John Stott, 'probably the most cruel
method of execution ever practised, for it deliberately delayed
death until maximum torture had been inflicted. The victim
could suffer for days before dying.'[2] Such was the disgrace,
disgust and horror associated with crucifixion that Roman

citizens were exempt, except for punishment for treason. In the words of Cicero, 'The mere mention of crucifixion was something unworthy of a Roman citizen and free man.'[3]

The world at large today, beginning with the Roman and Jewish world 2,000 years ago, finds it incredible that God himself would end his life on a cross. Such an idea was and is absurd. Was this just an over-zealous man accidently cut down in his prime? The first picture to survive of the crucifixion is a cartoon mocking it. It shows a man with a donkey's head, hanging on a cross, with a second man nearby raising his arm. The words beneath read: *Alexamenos cebete theon*, meaning 'Alexamenos worships God.'[4] In other words, the concept of worshipping a crucified God was tantamount to donkey-worship. And yet, through his own crucifixion, Jesus identified with human suffering on the deepest level.

Why me?

The pain of Jesus' last hours on earth was immense, but it was not the worst part. These dimensions of his suffering have been captured very dramatically and powerfully on film, but film has been unable to capture what made it so utterly awful for Jesus. Before he was arrested, he was clearly dreading something more, and prayed about it with such anxiety that blood began pouring through his sweat glands. This is a recognized physiological phenomenon that occurs under conditions of extreme stress, and presumably it is where we get the expression 'sweating blood' from. Was he purely dreading the prospect of physical pain and death? No. Many Christians have been horrifically tortured and martyred down through the ages, and have considered it a joy and privilege to suffer for God. Early Christians were subject to barbarities ranging from being roasted alive and eaten by lions, to crucifixion itself. They willingly endured such tortures because they considered what awaited them as infinitely more valuable even than life itself. Was Jesus any less brave than they were? Was he less willing to suffer and die? I think not. There was far more going on than Renaissance paintings and Hollywood movies can communicate. As he hung naked at a crossroads in Jerusalem, skewered through the hands and feet, Jesus experienced isolation on a cosmic scale. The land was plunged into darkness for the final three hours, perhaps depicting the spiritual darkness that had enveloped him. Jesus was bearing the blackness of our sin in his own body, so that we can know forgiveness and a relationship with our Maker once again. On the cross, separated from the light of his Father's face, he cried out, 'My God, my God, why have you forsaken me?' (Matthew 27:46). Jesus did not necessarily do this out of the same sense of bewilderment that we might experience. He knew what was happening. Yet at the same time it was agony.

What difference does this make today?

If you are asking, or have ever asked, 'Why me?', this question does not need to be suppressed. Jesus is not unfamiliar with 'Why?' questions, and, as we ask ours, they find an echo in Jesus' own experience. Here is a God you can go to, one who has not only suffered but has taken suffering to new unfathomable depths, and through his defeat of evil and death is able to pull us out of whatever depths we may find ourselves in. There is no pit too deep, because his was deeper still, no situation too God-forsaken, because his was the ultimate. Jesus is not aloof nor distant nor indifferent to your suffering. He is close to the broken-hearted and longs to comfort the grieving (2 Corinthians 1).[5] He is 'a man of suffering, and familiar with pain' (Isaiah 53:3). He cares deeply. He is listening. He is waiting. He has been waiting all your life.

The playlet entitled *The Long Silence* puts it well:

At the end of time, billions of people were scattered on a great plain before God's throne. Most shrank back from the brilliant light before them. But some groups near the front talked heatedly – not with cringing shame, but with belligerence. 'Can God judge us? How can he know about suffering?' snapped a pert young brunette. She ripped open a sleeve to reveal a tattooed number from a Nazi concentration camp. 'We endured terror . . . beatings . . . torture . . . death!' In another group a Negro boy lowered his collar. 'What about this?' he demanded, showing an ugly rope burn. 'Lynched . . . for no crime but being black!' In another crowd, a pregnant schoolgirl with sullen eyes. 'Why should I suffer?' she murmured. 'It wasn't my fault.'

Far out across the plain there were hundreds of such groups. Each had a complaint against God for the evil and suffering he permitted in this world. How lucky God was to live in heaven where all was sweetness and light, where there was no weeping or fear, no hunger or hatred. What did God know of all that man had been forced to endure in this world? For God leads a pretty sheltered life, they said. So each of these groups sent forth their leader, chosen because he had suffered the most. A Jew, a Negro, a person from Hiroshima, a horribly deformed arthritic, a thalidomide child. In the centre of the plain they consulted with each other. At last they were ready to present their case. It was rather clever.

Before God could be qualified to be their judge, he must endure what they had endured. Their decision was that God should be sentenced to live on earth – as a man! 'Let him be born a Jew. Let the legitimacy of his birth be doubted. Give him a work so difficult that even his family will think him out of his mind when he tries to do it. Let him be betrayed by his closest friends. Let him face false charges, be tried by a prejudiced jury and convicted by a cowardly judge. Let him be tortured. At the last, let him see what it means to be terribly alone. Then let him die. Let him die so there can be no doubt that he died. Let there be a great host of witnesses to verify it.' As each leader announced his portion of the sentence, loud murmurs of approval went up from the throng of people assembled. When the last had finished pronouncing sentence, there was a long silence. No-one uttered another word. No-one moved. For suddenly all knew that God had already served his sentence.[6]

6 Am I responsible for anyone else's suffering?

The financial crisis and subsequent recession have caused UK unemployment levels to rise to around 2.5 million, with hundreds of thousands losing their jobs every year. Many company CEOs and managers have had the unenviable task of breaking the devastating news to employees, for nobody wants to be the bearer of bad news. A family member worked in a company in which all employees were asked to take a pay cut of 10%, yet this was still not enough to get them through their difficulties. Engineers and administrators alike had to be made redundant, the majority of whom had hefty mortgages to pay, school uniforms to buy and families to feed. People were desperate to keep their jobs because there was little prospect of getting another. That workplace has seen some very sombre times, and there are no doubt thousands of others like it. The pressure upon company bosses is huge during prosperity, let alone during recession, and the burden of responsibility for their employees must be almost too much to bear. People in such positions must be all too well aware that they are very much responsible for the suffering of those they are letting go. The question at the beginning of this chapter may jar with you if you have ever found yourself in this position.

That said, the question: 'Am I responsible for anyone else's suffering?' is not one I have encountered when responding to people's queries about God. We seem to want to examine God's moral character, but never our own. All the other questions in this book have been frequently raised, and yet I think it is crucial to examine this less common one if we are to arrive at any concrete answers on suffering. When people think about suffering they tend to recall either situations in which they themselves have been wronged, or else wrongful acts by other people towards others. Rarely do we think about the suffering we ourselves may be causing, knowingly or otherwise.

Why is freedom so desirable?

In order to answer the question: 'Am I responsible for anyone else's suffering?' we need to return to the issue of freedom. In the West, living in freedom is viewed as one of the highest dignities a human being can enjoy. We uphold freedom of speech, freedom of expression, freedom of religion, and so on. But it is not restricted to democracy. We live in a culture that aspires to vast electronic freedom. Phone companies offer unlimited texts and phone minutes, essentially providing unlimited freedom to communicate. Free Wi-Fi provides us with unlimited freedom to roam the internet and connect with the world whenever and wherever we like. There is also a massive desire for financial freedom. Our life's aim is to become free to live, shop and holiday wherever we like, and to save enough to be worry-free in retirement. If we succeed, then we have truly arrived. An unspoken belief is that unlimited freedom offers the fullest possible life and the greatest possible happiness. That is what decent people are striving for. Why? And where does this desire for freedom come from?

Is God anti-freedom?

When people think about freedom, often the last place they look is towards God. Christianity is a list of dos and don'ts from a God who is restrictive, a party-pooper who spoils the fun. Yet the Bible says that right at the beginning, God gave an incredibly wide-ranging freedom to the very earliest humans in existence.

The verses that describe 'beginnings' are some of the most ancient literature that we have and also the subject of much debate. Christians hold a spectrum of different beliefs regarding how long ago these humans existed, the processes involved in their coming to exist and whether the Genesis accounts are to be taken literally or figuratively. A point of overlap is that at some stage humans had a 'high point' and were given a unique capacity and freedom to relate to God. But Christians do differ on whether this 'high point' was attained gradually or endowed from the beginning.

The traditional view is that these first humans, whom the Bible calls Adam and Eve, began at this 'high point'. They lived in an incredible freedom, experiencing contentment and happiness with each other and with God. They were free to go anywhere and do and eat anything: 'You are free to eat from any tree in the garden' (Genesis 2:16). God is not anti-freedom today, nor was he in those early days of existence. In fact, one could argue that freedom gained its very definition from that time.

Freedom lost

There was only one limit on freedom; these humans were to avoid one tree: 'You are free to eat from any tree in the garden, but you must not eat from the tree of the knowledge of good and evil, for when you eat from it you will certainly die' (Genesis 2:16–17). This is not God taking delight in 'dangling' quite literally forbidden fruit. This is the means by which God established humans as moral beings able to choose between right and wrong. As we saw earlier, for moral freedom to be real there must always be the option of choosing the wrong. The tree represented this moral choice, and it was costly.

The misunderstanding that God opposes enjoyment is ancient in its origin; indeed the suggestion was first made to this couple. The enemy of God, Satan, represented by a serpent, was in the garden as well. We do not know the specifics of how he came to be there, but a real possibility of evil would have been needed for humans to make a real moral choice. Here we are reminded of the concept introduced in chapter 1 that evil is not just the absence of good, but also a personal being, the devil.

In the West the topic of Satan can often seem excessive and generate a feeling of discomfort. The devil features frequently in the vernacular, but rarely in serious conversation. Our children's programmes and literature are packed full of battles between good and evil, as though this knowledge is paramount at an early age, yet it is viewed with scepticism in adulthood. On the other hand, the market for films involving dark spiritual forces, such as *The Exorcist*, continues to thrive. Many individuals also participate in séances to contact the dead, or even in satanic rituals, so much so that Satanism has become an established belief system worldwide. C. S. Lewis summarized our approach to the devil clearly:

> There are two equal and opposite errors into which our race can fall about the devils. One is to disbelieve in their existence. The other is to believe, and to feel an excessive and unhealthy interest in them. They themselves are equally pleased by both errors and hail a materialist or a magician with the same delight.[1]

Christianity holds that Satan is real and ultimately behind the atrocities in our world. His aim is to oppose the purposes of God, summarized well in Jesus' own words: 'The thief [Satan] comes only to *steal* and *kill* and *destroy*; I have come that they may have life, and have it to the full' (John 10:10; emphasis mine). Some who have been caught up in atrocities such as the Rwandan genocide testified to a tangible presence of evil amid the theft, death and destruction. However, the Bible does not describe good and evil as equal and opposite forces battling it out. Satan entered after the universe was started; he is part of the created world and therefore is subject to God. Some passages suggest he was created good but fell from grace, causing a corruption of his own nature and ultimately enticing humans to follow suit.

The serpent distorted God's words: 'Did God really say, "You must not eat from *any* tree in the garden"?'(Genesis 3:1; emphasis mine). As apologist John Lennox phrases it, God is suddenly accused of forbidding access to *all* trees! The serpent caused Adam and Eve to question God's reliability. Had God told them the whole story? Or was he withholding some greater level of freedom? 'You will not certainly die . . . for God knows that when you eat [the forbidden fruit] your eyes will be opened, and you will be like God, knowing good and evil' (Genesis 3:4–5).

Suspicion and distrust of God was now roused. Adam and Eve believed the serpent and used their moral freedom to ignore God and establish their independence from him, entering into what they thought was a greater freedom. How wrong they were. This decision disconnected them from God. A relationship previously marked by love and closeness was now dominated by fear, isolation and hiding:

> Then the man and his wife heard the sound of the LORD God as he was walking in the garden . . . and they hid from the LORD God among the trees of the garden. But the LORD God called to the man, 'Where are you?'
> He answered, 'I heard you in the garden, and I was afraid because I was naked; so I hid.'
> (Genesis 3:8–10)

They were no longer free, but confined and afraid. A flawed aspect to human nature was introduced that caused immediate fractures in other areas of life too. The first realization was utter nakedness and, with it, shame. A discontentment with oneself and a need to cover up or put on a façade were introduced. The relationship to each other moved from being one of love and equality to one of blame, arguments and male domination. The impact of this 'fall' on the natural world is another area in which Christians differ. For some, it was at this point that natural disasters were introduced. The natural world changed from being stable to being unstable and hostile, subject to death and decay. Others hold that tectonic plates had been moving and volcanoes erupting for a long time, but what has changed since the 'fall' has been our connectedness to the natural world. (We will examine these perspectives in more detail in the next chapter.)

Why is this still relevant today?

Why are these ancient events relevant? Precisely because they are still prevalent today. We have not become morally refined as a race with the passage of time. The revolutions of industry, technology, medicine, modern science and modern communication have greatly improved life quality, but they have done nothing to improve our morality. If anything, our behaviour is worse than ever. Christians hold that this decision to reject God has somehow introduced a blueprint for the entire human race, such that every human being encounters these same disconnects. We may not fully understand how we could inherit this nature down through the generations, but if our DNA is inherited and can be traced back, then why not other aspects of our nature and social and moral practice as well?

We have not become morally refined as a race with the passage of time.

Unlimited freedom leading to restriction

In the West we have been exposed to a great deal of monetary freedom. Interest rates have been low, and until recently borrowing was easy. So in theory, the utopia of unlimited financial freedom arrived for some. Why then are we not still enjoying that freedom? Some of us know all too well that the freedom to borrow given to us by banks and building societies ended up being destructive. People borrowed more than they could afford and landed themselves and their families in debt. As a result of large-scale unlimited monetary freedom, the West experienced the biggest financial crisis since the 1920s. Are we freer as a result? Of course not. It is now very difficult to borrow and acquire credit; the housing market is slow; and cuts in public spending are being made across the political board to begin to pay off our debts as a nation. More concerning is the fact that people are buckling under the pressure of debt. Debt has led to relationship breakdowns, caused many to live in daily fear of the future and driven some to consider suicide. What is the bottom line here? Why has seemingly unlimited financial freedom had such a destructive impact on us as a nation? Could this be a modern-day example of an ancient problem?

Why is it that human beings are capable of being both lovers and rapists, home-makers and home looters, generous with our money and yet extracting it illegally from the state? Why is it that, after a disaster such as an earthquake or tsunami, the donations flood in, and yet each time there are also scam agencies preying on people's generosity and pocketing the money themselves? How is it that computers with incredible capabilities have been invented, and yet we also need to install anti-virus software to protect them against sabotage?

How is it that some people volunteer to donate organs after they die, in order to help someone else live, while others are stabbing or shooting in the streets with the express aim of helping people die? Why is it that so many of us live with guilt and regrets, things we did or said in the past that we wish we hadn't but are now powerless to change? Why is it that there are so many good things we would love to teach our children, yet we never seem to need to teach them jealousy or selfishness or greed? In fact, much of our energy is spent teaching them the opposite: to share, to listen, to be patient and kind.

Why is it that we lock our doors and windows at night? In some parts of the 'free' world there are bars on the windows and even at the tops of the stairs. Why is it that we always need a receipt to return goods to a shop or to show a ticket before boarding a train? The reason is that people cannot be trusted. A person's word is not always reliable. Proof must be provided. We protest when short-changed, but keep silent when given too much.

In writing a book on evil, there is sadly no shortage of material. There is something fundamentally good and noble about humans, but also something fundamentally flawed, and it is endemic to life. We are not able to handle our God-given freedom correctly, and as a result could well be responsible for suffering, be it of a serious or more minor nature. The Bible calls this inherited 'flawedness' sin.

But I am a good person

Sin is such a loaded word. A common sentiment when discussing sin is: 'I am a good person. I have lived a good life and haven't done anything wrong.' The concept of sin and seemingly falling short in some way can cause offence. What 'I am a good person' usually means is: 'I have lived a moral life and have not committed murder, adultery, child abuse, robbery or any of the major crimes that disrupt society. I don't drink too much, I don't sleep around, I don't smoke, I try not to swear. Overall, a pretty good upstanding citizen.' This is no bad thing, but Christianity isn't about trying to be a better person by avoiding certain activities. Sadly, Jesus' diagnosis suggests that the situation is much more serious than that. Trying to become 'good' by avoiding illicit acts is merely papering over the cracks of the human condition. The truth is that nobody is capable of being good by just trying harder. In order to become 'good', we need a radical change of heart. Jesus was once addressed as good: 'Good teacher, what must I do to inherit eternal life?', and he returned the question with another: 'Why do you call me good? No one is good – except God alone' (Luke 18:18). The implication is that goodness is defined in terms of being like God. Who then qualifies? Michael Ramsden puts it well: 'Think about this: if you have to be good to go to heaven and only God is good, who is going? God and . . . no one else. In other words, Jesus is saying, "Your application to join the Trinity has been refused."'[2] We may try to be good, but ultimately can't even live up to our own standards.

But I can become 'good' by trying harder

So there is a problem, but our natural tendency is to solve it ourselves by trying harder, working harder, reading more books, and so on. Our shops have whole sections dedicated to 'Self-help', offering solutions. Advice ranges from aromatherapy to homeopathy, from massage to psychology and meditation. The hypnotist and best-selling author Paul McKenna has written books on many subjects: *I Can Make You Happy*, *I Can Make You Thin*, *I Can Make You Sleep*, *Instant Confidence*, *Change Your Life in Seven Days* and *Control Stress*. People are drawn to these titles because of a desire to fix our problems and to fix them *ourselves*. Mahatma Gandhi once said, 'You cannot change the world. Change yourself and you change your world. Be the change you want to see in the world.' There is some truth here in that changing the world does begin with each individual. But the Christian message is that we are not able to effect change without radical help from outside ourselves. Changing the world begins by becoming 'good' from God's perspective, and this is made possible not by doing moral things, for it cannot be earned, but by being forgiven.

A scene from Jesus' life describes how the religious leaders were criticizing his followers for not rigidly obeying the Jewish custom of ceremonially washing their hands before eating. The religious leaders' belief was that failing to wash one's hands would render the food, and therefore the person, 'unclean' before God. Jesus responds by saying,

> Nothing outside a person can defile them by going into them. Rather, it is what comes out of a person that defiles them . . . What comes out of a person is what defiles them. For it is from within, out of a person's heart, that evil thoughts come – sexual immorality, theft, murder, adultery, greed, malice, deceit, lewdness, envy, slander, arrogance and folly. All these evils come from inside and defile a person.
> (Mark 7:15, 20–23)

The symptoms listed by Jesus are wide-ranging. Commit murder or theft, and you may well end up in prison. Commit adultery or sexual immorality, and you may well end up on YouTube. Greed, envy and arrogance however are much more subtle. They can be invisible. Indeed you could be guilty of these, but no-one except you need ever know. Jesus says that all these things, although very different, have the same cause: a person whose will, mind, emotions and thoughts are hardened towards God, saying or thinking, 'I don't need you, God. I can manage just fine on my own. I can do it my way.'

One of the most popular songs at funerals at the moment is Frank Sinatra's song 'My Way'. It is an incredibly grand song with powerful lyrics. And yet it is bittersweet. Some who insist on living life 'their way' can leave a path of rubble behind them. The song is grand and fun for the singer, but not so much fun for the listener. Yes, many of us live life 'our way', but who have we trampled on in the process? Contrary to popular understanding, there is only one root Sin with a capital 'S' and that is to echo the decision of those first humans and say to God, 'I'm doing it "My Way".' Sin is not just general, but personal. Each individual has a choice of whether they will trust God or reject him. Because of this the problem of evil is not just out there in the world; it is in here too. Evil is internal as well as external.

But why am I responsible for evil? Surely God is responsible?

Many find it grossly unfair that they are doomed from birth because of the actions of two people thousands of years ago. After all, we did not ask to be born into a flawed human race. Why are we declared guilty before we can even speak? Surely God is ultimately responsible for setting up the conditions that made our rebellion possible, rather than shifting the blame onto people? He created the free world, discussed in chapter 3, which included moral freedom, so he is responsible for what happened next.

This is a valid question. If I were God and in the process of creating people and their habitat, would I have set things up so beautifully and then given them the option to walk away, if they so wished? Knowing the consequence of that choice, if they took it? I don't know. I can barely imagine it with my own children, let alone the entire human race. The honest answer to this question is, yes, God has made a world where evil is possible, but this still does not detract from the decision of humans to make evil *actual*. People were given the costly dignity of moral freedom so that genuine love could be possible, as discussed in chapter 3, and with it a weighty responsibility to use freedom wisely. We did not, and there were grave consequences. For God to allow a world with the *potential* for evil remains distinct from the actions of humans that made evil a *reality*.

Even so, God himself was prepared to step inside the very conditions that he created in order to provide a solution to this human condition. He did not wait for us to clean up. God took the initiative in the rescue operation and sent his Son, so that 'while we were still sinners, Christ died for us' (Romans 5:8). One of St Paul's letters to the church in Rome describes a connection between this first man, Adam, and Jesus: the first introduced the problem, the latter provided the solution. As the person of Jesus Christ, God stepped into human history and allowed himself to be 'destroyed' by evil and through that process somehow to dethrone it.

> Therefore, just as sin entered the world through one man, and death through sin, and in this way death came to all people, because all sinned . . . But the gift is not like the trespass. For if the many died by the trespass of the one man, how much more did God's grace and the gift that came by the grace of the one man, Jesus Christ, overflow to the many! . . . Consequently, just as one trespass resulted in condemnation for all people, so also one righteous act resulted in justification and life for all people. For just as through the disobedience of the one man the many were made sinners, so also through the obedience of the one man the many will be made righteous.
>
> (Romans 5:12, 15, 18–19)

During a particularly difficult episode of my husband's illness we were at a very low ebb and speaking to a friend about what to do. My friend said, 'Sometimes you can't fight it. You have to go with it, go down underneath it and let God bring you back up again.' This is exactly what Jesus did on our behalf. He who had no evil in him willingly stepped into an evil world, with all its profanity and grit and blood and death and sickness and power struggles and stress, and willingly allowed himself to be destroyed by evil. He went down underneath it, so that the power of sin could be broken and the human condition reversed. All without destroying our freedom.

In the line of fire

Many who were alive at the time can remember where they were and what they were doing on 22 November 1963. This was the day when John F. Kennedy was assassinated in Dallas, Texas. Clint Hill was one of two secret service agents especially noted for his bravery on that day. He has recently published his memoirs[3] and recalls in them, after an almost fifty-year silence, how events unfolded. Mr Hill was running alongside the vehicle behind the President's car when the first shot was fired. His job was to protect the First Lady, Jackie Kennedy, so he began running towards the President's car in front. Two further shots were fired at President Kennedy, the second of which proved to be fatal. Hill, by now in the President's car, threw himself on top of Mrs Kennedy to protect her. He placed himself in the line of fire so that any further bullets would impact his body instead of hers. Mr Hill was recently interviewed and asked about the cost of having a job where you must be prepared to die for the protection of others. He responded that it is as though you must consider the other's life as more valuable, more important, than your own. Not everyone is willing to pay such a price for another, but Clint Hill was and he may well have saved Jackie Kennedy's life in the process.

On the cross Jesus willingly placed himself in the firing line on our behalf. He considered our lives, our freedom, as more important than his own. Clint Hill did not need to take any bullets, but Jesus took into his body the whole artillery of hell. Everything Satan had to fire at him was unleashed. On the cross Jesus was riddled with all of the sins ever committed, the thing he had been dreading most before his death, because God the Father cannot look at someone full of sin. Jesus was forsaken by his dearly loved Father, and darkness, evil and aloneness prevailed. I wonder if he glimpsed deep depression during these hours. You see, beatings, floggings and crucifixion are horrific enough even if God is with you, comforting and strengthening you. But Jesus endured this while cut off from the Father that he had known for all eternity, which took his suffering to a cosmic level.

Jesus forfeited his closeness with the Father, so that when we suffer we never need be alone. Jesus allowed himself to be destroyed by evil for a time, so that evil need never destroy us. Jesus was forsaken by God, so that we never have to be when we suffer. Jesus took the bullets intended for us so that we can go free. In fact, he used his freedom to save us, without removing our own freedom. We are free to ask him for forgiveness, for new life, for his comforting presence when we suffer, or we are still free to say, 'No, thank you'.

The Bible describes what happened on the cross as an exchange between us and God: 'God made him who had no sin to be sin for us, so that in him we might become the righteousness of God' (2 Corinthians 5:21). Jesus who had no sin took on our sin, and we who had much sin took on a God nature that makes us right before God again. We needed someone who was like us, in other words human, but also not like us, in other words born without the stain of human sin. Only one person in all history has ever met both criteria: Jesus Christ, fully God and fully human.

But why can't God just forgive and forget?

The atheist Richard Dawkins strongly disagrees with the need for any action to deal with human sin, asserting, 'If God wanted to forgive our sins, why not just forgive them, without having himself tortured and executed in payment . . . ?'[4] Perhaps others can identify with this question. Wasn't Jesus' death at best a bit excessive and at worst sadistic? If God is so bent on forgiving, then why not just forgive and be done with it? Why put to death an innocent person in the process?

A question like this does not take full account of the reality and seriousness of sin, nor the costliness of forgiveness. If someone has been attacked, and the police decide to ignore it and do nothing, there would be outrage from the victim and a potential rise in crime as other opportunists tried their luck. Equally, forgiving a wrongdoer is not an easy or light-hearted process. It is painful and costly. In the words of Tim Keller, 'no-one "just" forgives if the evil is serious'.[5] Just letting people off the hook is equivalent to saying that what they did doesn't matter, and the victim isn't important either. But it does matter, and just as breaking the law of the land incurs a penalty, so does sin. Asking God to ignore wrongdoing is asking him for less love, not more.

In the book of Hebrews we read that 'without the shedding of blood there is no forgiveness of sins' (Hebrews 9:22). In other words, the nature of sin is so serious that in order to deal with it blood must be spilt. Elsewhere we see that 'the wages of sin is death' (Romans 6:23). In other words, if you work at sin, the payment you get back is death: relational death, self-worth death, physical death, spiritual death, eternal death. Christians do not delight in being solemn for its own sake. But sin is serious, and to deal with it something or someone had to die. Prior to Jesus, the people of God used to make atonement through animal sacrifices, until Jesus himself chose to be that someone, providing a permanent, once-and-for-all sacrifice, hence the term 'Lamb of God'. But he was not strung up as a helpless victim or scapegoat. God did not punish his Son with our sins. No, God stepped into history himself as Jesus and willingly chose to die. There is a difference. He spoke of his death in this way, long before it happened: 'No one takes [my life] from me, but I lay it down of my own accord. I have authority to lay it down and authority to take it up again' (John 10:18).

Aren't Christians just obsessed with sin and death?

A common objection is that Christians are too obsessed with sin and death, and that focusing on these puts too much of a negative slant on things. Those in the East would say that sin, and its consequence: death, portrays people in an unnecessarily bad light. In the West we hear it too. The *Times* columnist Robert Crampton voices this complaint in the context of a school nativity play:

> I do love a Christmas carol, the tunes, naturally, but also the words, so much more optimistic than the doom-laden death-cult lyrics served up in many hymns the rest of the year. Except the last verse of 'We Three Kings', an otherwise jaunty number, is always a bit of a downer, especially when sung by some adorable kid with her whole life ahead of her: 'Myrrh is mine, its bitter perfume / Breathes of life of gathering gloom / Sorrowing, sighing, bleeding, dying / Sealed in a stone-cold tomb' . . . When is the penny going to drop with Christianity? Death, martyrdom, suffering, pain, loss, blood, these are not concepts with which any brand would want to be identified. If that's the core of your message, no wonder you've got a problem.[6]

The question is: does the Christian diagnosis of the human condition ring true or not? Does it help you make sense of life or not? The solution to sin is not pretty, because the disease is fairly ugly as well. Christianity does not focus on sin for its own sake, but rather offers a correct diagnosis of the problem before then offering a solution. My husband's illness had the doctors running all sorts of tests. He was given lumbar punctures, EEGs, ECGs, MRIs, various drugs, and so on, to get to the bottom of it. When someone is seriously ill it is only right that identifying the problem should take all of our energy until an accurate diagnosis is reached. Not so that the diagnosis can be wallowed in, but so that steps can be taken to restore normal life.

Wouldn't it be incredible to get back to the levels of freedom enjoyed by those earliest humans?

So can we enjoy restored freedom?

Recognizing sin is not the end-point for the Christian, but the beginning of restored freedom. Robert Crampton was right about the penultimate verse of 'We Three Kings', but he forgot to look at the final verse:

Glorious now behold Him arise,
King and God and Sacrifice.
Alleluia, alleluia!
Sounds through the earth and skies.

Jesus did not remain in the grave, but was raised to life. Evil, sin and death had gripped Jesus for a time, but they could not hold him down for long. Jesus is God. God is indestructible life. So death's hold over Jesus was temporary. Three days afterwards he burst into life again. People like to say that Jesus came back to life, but it is truer to say that he went through death and out the other side, never to die again. Theologians and philosophers and even lawyers have debated the empty tomb for millennia. The authorities were never able to produce a body; hundreds claimed to have seen the risen Jesus; and his petrified followers became bold and courageous leaders with an incredible story. Virtually overnight they were suddenly prepared to die for their faith. Something extraordinary had indeed happened.

Jesus' life, death and resurrection are not just interesting historical events from 2,000 years ago. They have immeasurable relevance today. Just as the consequences of Adam and Eve's disobedience seem to prevail today, so too can the events of Jesus' life, death and resurrection be appropriated in individual lives. He can break the influence of evil, sin and death, not only when your physical body gives up, but also in your daily life today. He can break patterns of behaviour that we have tried for years to conquer but with no success. He can reconcile families, defuse anger, release guilt, heal remorse. Exactly how this is possible is difficult to rationalize. Can I explain it? No. Are there equations to prove it? No. But I and countless others can tell you that it is true and objectively real in our own lives, and it begins with our free choice. Jesus says, 'Because I live, you also will live' (John 14:19). But you need to ask.

I finish this chapter as I began, with the question of freedom. How can we live in the freedom that we long for? Wouldn't it be great to get back to our original freedom? Is such a thing even possible? Yes, it is. But in an unexpected way. True freedom is found not by removing all boundaries, but by changing the human heart and living within God-given ones. This is what was meant by Jesus' words: 'If the Son [Jesus] sets you free, you will be free indeed' (John 8:36). Our desire for freedom is God-given. Jesus came to bring it. Though we look for it in so many other empty places, the fullest form of freedom that it is possible to have is precisely within God's fold, not outside of it. It is a freedom made real by Jesus Christ himself.

Our desire for freedom is God-given. Jesus came to bring it.

We are not responsible for the global human problem, nor are we responsible for its solution. These things are far bigger than us and have been dealt with on our behalf on a level beyond our understanding. But we are responsible for whether or not we will freely accept Jesus and his ability to change the human heart today, and bring an end to any suffering for which we are responsible. So the question remains: how will we use our freedom?

Charles's story

We arrived in Somalia to find anarchy. You couldn't even have called it war; it was just chaos, lawlessness and starvation. It was September 1993, just one month before the infamous Black Hawk Down incident. Such was the danger that when our plane touched down at Mogadishu airport, the pilot kept the engine running. As soon as we had jumped off, the ladder was hoisted back up again and the plane prepared for take-off. Within minutes it was back in the sky.

We learned that the beautiful ocean was notorious for sharks and the lovely strip of grass in front of the pristine sand contained landmines. In the airport itself there were young guys with guns shooting spasmodically. It wasn't long before we noticed that bits of concrete were coming off the walls as shots landed close to us. We fell to the ground, crawled out and were met by colleagues in trucks with anti-aircraft guns on top. They called them 'technicals'. These men took us to a place of safety under armed escort. It was the only way to survive.

We went past what had been the American Embassy and were able to walk around the compound because the wall had been blown to pieces. The buildings were derelict and burned out. We found ourselves paddling through piles of paper, mostly children's school books and colouring books, plus little toys and bits of school furniture.

We walked past the hospitals and entered one that had been abandoned. It was a stinking place with bloodstained floors and decrepit scenes. We could smell sewage in some rooms. It was awful. People would have been healthier staying out of it. And that was the hospital.

Stray bullets were a risk on the streets. Young men drove around in cars with guns sticking out of the windows which they fired intermittently. Partly it was out of exuberance, partly boredom, and also because they were chewing a leaf called qat, a mild narcotic that made them spacey and staved off hunger. Five minutes did not pass without the sound of gunshots somewhere. In the marketplaces you could buy a Kalashnikov, and a box of bullets or a grenade for the price of a loaf of bread.

I've worked in and with various NGOs, and at that time I was with an international relief and development organization. The suffering was becoming serious. The majority of people were unable to farm, couldn't grow food, couldn't even get food, so they were at starvation levels, and the main aid convoys hadn't really moved in yet. We spent some days working with the aid responses. We moved to a refugee camp, an NGO feeding station for people trying to flee the fighting. In aid terms, a feeding station is a disaster. Nobody wants it. But people had walked for weeks to get there, and you have to do something urgently or they will die.

At this place there were 4,000 people lining up and quietly waiting for food. It was bizarre because, while people queued, some of our NGO colleagues were playing games with children and the parents were joining in. People sang songs and the atmosphere became lighter. They would dance around, stand on their heads and make other visual jokes. Suddenly, in the midst of all their suffering, there was joking and laughter, spontaneously amongst those who had nothing and were waiting for food. You could almost sense a bit of normality, but then you realized that these completely destitute people would starve to death unless they soon found food.

A mother walked into the camp, carrying a baby very close to her chest wrapped in a blanket. I asked how many children she had. She said two and that they were twins. Normally we expected to hear stories of five, six or ten, but she was young. We asked where the other child was. It had died two or three weeks earlier while she had been walking to find this feeding centre, and she had been walking ever since. There was no burial for the baby. My colleagues asked if they could examine the child she was carrying, and she very tenderly unwrapped it from her chest. But this one too had died. I realized that she had probably walked for days or weeks with a dead baby. But I don't think she had enough energy to show emotion or cry. She was as thin as a rake, clearly starving and very thirsty. She was able to tell us that the twin had already died but she couldn't bring herself to say that this one was gone too.

A day or two later we were in a similar area, this time with a convoy of food. It was under UN support, so there were helicopters above to protect us and vehicles with guns all around our trucks. We arrived at a village and began to look at the food distribution. It was all extremely well organized by the local elders of the community and running smoothly. But somehow in our efficiency we had not looked beyond a hundred metres. I noticed something on the ground and went over to look at what seemed like a pile of rags. A UN soldier came with me. We got to the rags and saw that this was in fact a person, a twelve- to fourteen-year-old girl. Her name was Walia. I realized that she was breathing, but very slowly.

The soldier opened his water flask and dribbled some over her face, and she drank some. After a few minutes she opened her eyes and was able to sit up with our help. We gave her more water, and another colleague came and interpreted for us. It turned out that she was sick and trying to find a health clinic. 'Clinic' is too fancy a word. It was just a place under a tree with a local nurse. This girl was only a matter of metres from the clinic, probably thirty seconds to a minute away. It was now within sight, but she couldn't manage the last few steps and had just collapsed. We were able to carry her to safety and were told she would certainly have died right there if we hadn't stopped and found her. I realized that spotting a pile of rags, discovering it was a human being and realizing that all she needed was food, water and basic medicine represented the difference between life and death.

Life was fragile. Whereas the first woman had walked for weeks with incredible discipline, this young girl had given up and would have breathed her last if we hadn't noticed her. I felt guilty, wondering how often I had missed such small signs of life – and am I responsible for these things? I began to get frantic and look and look and look, keeping my eyes open, and listening, trying to be everywhere all at once, feeling more and more responsible, but of course it's impossible. I often thought about that girl: 'Would she ever know who it was who had helped her?' A photographer took a picture of the three of us – the soldier, the girl and me – and it was published in a Kenyan newspaper.

The next story is similar. It was in one of the feeding stations which had been functioning for a while. People were beginning to gain strength, and some were heading back into the villages, which was to be encouraged. Families were getting back on their feet, beginning to find relatives in the crowd and planning their way out of the crisis. So I was doing a very different kind of interviewing, listening to people telling me about their dreams and future plans. I walked around a bush, bringing an interpreter with me, and there in the shade was a very quiet older man with yet another pile of rags beside him on the ground and what I thought was a four-year-old boy, crouched over, kind of bent double. I discovered that the 'rags' were in fact the mother who had died that morning. They hadn't yet had the strength to bury her, even though this was quite against their traditional ways and against all common sense in that hot climate, and so we got help to make sure that she was properly buried.

For a few minutes I sat with the boy and through the interpreter began to ask him about himself. I discovered that he wasn't four or five at all, not even nine or ten. He was in fact eighteen. That's what starvation does: it strips away the body, removes all flesh. This skeletal boy who looked so young and tiny was in fact a young adult without the strength to stand up. We brought him some water, and I continued asking him about the future.

'What is your dream?' I asked.

Without hesitating he said, 'I dream of being a farmer.'

I said, 'What kind of farmer, and how will you do it?'

He began to describe exactly the sort of farm he wanted, the sort of farming he would do and how he'd plan it. He had all this in his mind and was clearly intending to do it. We talked for a little while longer, and then he fell very silent. To my dismay, he sort of leant forward again, bent double, and when we tried to lift him up he was no longer breathing. We were unable to revive him, and he died right there. I had my arm around him when he died. His shoulder was so spindly and thin that it was almost painful to touch. It was an alarming experience, but I kept my hand there for a while.

I had a very different feeling about that boy than about the others because he had actually died talking about his dream. For a very sick person, he was almost animated. He kept repeating, 'If God wills, if God wills'. He talked about his dreams, if God wills. Of course that's just a turn of phrase, and I have heard it thousands of times when working in Muslim cultures. But this boy was thinking about his future and he was relating it to God. Probably the effort of telling the story was the last drain on his body, and he just couldn't sustain it. I felt guilty about that. I wondered if I had hastened his death in some way. A colleague helped me to remember that it wasn't about me; it was about him. And now we needed to be concerned about the family.

It wasn't long before we moved out of that area. I felt great reluctance and I thought about him a lot. This boy was not concentrating on his needs, or his sicknesses, or his starvation, or his thirst, or his lack of clothing, or lack of shelter, or his own bereavement, or his destitution. He was actually planning his future, in a positive frame of mind, and was very, very glad to talk. He really wanted to talk to somebody and was happy to talk to me, a stranger.

I can't possibly imagine the suffering that these people had gone through. But even though they were suffering severely, they seemed to cope in different ways. Some were angry, while some were morose and quiet and gave up, and some were animated and positive and could even laugh and joke. Having worked in international development for much of my life, I have seen some of the world's worst situations: catastrophes, disasters, earthquakes, floods, wars, violence, and everything else you could imagine. These stories, and many others, speak to me of there being something wrong with the world and of the need to intervene not only in the short term, but to seek solutions in the long term too.

The older I grow, the harder it becomes to put suffering into tidy boxes. There's something very mysterious and something very individual and personal about it. When I was surrounded by suffering I experienced a strange dichotomy. My emotions were calm, but in my mind I was shouting at God, 'Where were you when all this happened? Why do you let some people suffer so much?' But after I had returned home and sat reflecting in our peaceful garden, my reasoning became all neat and tidy again, while my emotions fell apart. I sobbed, laughed or just fell silent, and often longed to go back to be closer to the people.

Later my wife and I were able to live and work in Jerusalem. We learned from Christians in the West Bank and Gaza that, despite prolonged suffering, it is possible to have both peace in your heart and consistency in your reasoning at the same time. They have processed suffering in this way for generations, but that's another story.

7 Why does God allow natural disasters and diseases?

On 26 December 2004, millions watched their TV screens in disbelief as a wall of water surged onto beaches in Thailand, Indonesia and southern India, killing upwards of 250,000 people and destroying homes, livelihoods and entire families. In March 2011 Japan was struck by a massive earthquake and tsunami that devastated miles and miles of coastline towns, leaving 20,000 dead or missing. Parts of Haiti were devastated in an earthquake in 2009, as was Aquila, Italy in 2008. In 2005 Hurricane Katrina decimated New Orleans and many other cities and neighbourhoods in Mississippi, Alabama and Florida. We can barely go a couple of months without hearing of a new disaster.

How do we make sense of natural disasters such as these? Even if people are responsible for their actions, we cannot be responsible for cataclysmic events. They are caused by forces so much bigger than us. Humans, far from being the cause, are swept away by such things. Our insurance policies protect us against 'acts of God'. Is this what they are? How can God allow so many innocent people to die in these so-called 'acts'? Why does he let them happen?

The questions do not stop here. What about the impact of disease and sickness? We may not necessarily have been caught up in a natural disaster, but we have all, in one way or another, encountered illness. Is there a family in the Western world that *hasn't* encountered the dreaded 'c' word? As the average age of our populations increases, diseases such as cancer, Alzheimer's and dementia are on the rise. At the other end of the life scale we encounter diseases such as childhood leukaemia, meningitis and scarlet fever. In between infanthood and old age we could suffer anything from eczema to arthritis, from hay fever to organ failure, and from anaemia to a heart attack. Disease and sickness range from minor complaints to the debilitating or fatal. Sickness seems to be part of life, and yet time and time again we find ourselves asking, 'Why is life full of disease and sickness?' or 'Why am I suffering from this illness?'

Philosophers refer to both natural disasters and diseases as 'natural evil'. In other words, evil that impacts the natural world itself, either through geophysics in the case of natural disasters or through our biology in the case of disease. There are a number of different explanations for 'natural evil'. Since in the West the way that we encounter suffering through natural disasters differs from how we encounter suffering through sickness, I will address these two forms of natural evil separately.

What about diseases and sickness?

A popular response is that a world riddled with disease and sickness is simply the way the world is. The very process of evolution involves weeding out weaker genes and preserving the stronger ones. So genes mutate, diseases arise, and some people are affected, whereas others aren't. Survival of the fittest if you like. Passionate atheists such as Richard Dawkins have put it even more bleakly:

In a universe of blind physical forces and genetic replication, some people are going to get hurt, other people are going to get lucky, and you won't find any rhyme or reason in it, nor any justice. The universe we observe has precisely the properties we should expect if there is, at bottom, no design, no purpose, no evil and no good, nothing but blind pitiless indifference.[1]

The Christian response would be that this is not just the way the world is. There is a brokenness at the level of our physical bodies that has not always been present. When people said 'no' to God they also dragged along into their rebellion their very skin and bones, their very heart and brain, their very muscles and marrow. It is as though our disconnect from God entered the physicality of every person ever to live, whether religious or irreligious. But in general when someone becomes ill, be it with a common cold or terminal cancer, it is not necessarily a personal punishment from God. No, it is a general consequence of living in a world in which our very bodies are not as they should be because humankind is out of sync with their Maker.

Atheism – Human beings are the solution
Either way, whether theist or atheist, we agree that human beings have a part to play in combatting suffering, but for very different reasons. Atheists would hold that precisely because this world is all there is and there are no other forces at play, humans must do all they can to remedy the suffering of others. In other words, the solution to the problem of pain is people. We ourselves must fight evil. There is no-one else to help, so we must play our part, and we do so by developing medicine to fight disease and disaster prediction technology to limit natural disasters. As one nineteenth-century author put it, 'I do not believe in God . . . But I believe in Man. In man's redeeming power; in man's remoulding energy; in man's approaching triumph, through knowledge, love and work.'[2] The Secular Humanist Manifesto of 2000 describes hope in human ability

in this way: 'For the first time in human history [people] possess the means provided by science and technology to ameliorate the human condition, advance happiness and freedom, and enhance human life for all people on this planet.'[3] Human beings are the solution.

Theism – God is the solution through human beings

The theist would say that people have a role to play in relieving suffering as an expression of an incredibly noble side to human nature that was given to those first humans, and as a means of repairing the brokenness that was introduced when those first humans rejected God. In other words, we want to help people, whether we believe in God or not, because we are made by a God who wants to help people. God is not indifferent to human illness, nor is he inactive. He intervenes in human illness through other people, through the discoveries of medicine and technology, and through the tireless work of nurses, doctors, therapists, social workers, counsellors, aid workers and NGOs. Christians would say that the very existence of these professions and their discoveries speaks of a God who cares about human illness and intervenes indirectly through other people.

Many assume that science and the medical advances it yields are necessarily atheistic, but the foundations on which science rests call this into question. Science proceeds on the basis that there is order both in nature and in the human mind, which Christians believe is because they are both derived from the same Creator.[4] We not only believe that God is pro-science and pro-technology, but that he is the very basis on which they are made possible. Modern medicine and technology therefore are part of the way in which God intervenes in human illness. He shows his compassion for the sick through the discoveries and actions of other people.

This does not mean of course that if our illness is poorly diagnosed or untreatable that God has forgotten us. It reminds us of the complexity of the human body and the limitations of the human beings who try to make sense of it. Science cannot solve every problem. We cannot 'enhance human life for all people', as secular humanists would have it. Untreatable illness is a reminder of the brevity and fragility of human life. Perhaps it raises questions about the bigger picture. Is this life all there is? The Bible speaks of a God who is close to the broken-hearted, who does not disregard the weak, who strengthens the weary and who points us to a bigger story beyond our own. (More about this in chapter 8: 'Can a broken story be fixed?')

Lifestyle impacts health

Many will recall the movie *Supersize Me* in which film maker Morgan Spurlock investigated obesity in Americans by eating only food from McDonald's for an entire month. Spurlock had to eat three meals a day, consume everything on the McDonald's menu at least once and, when asked if he would like to 'supersize' his meal order, he had to accept. In addition, Spurlock did not exercise during this period and limited his movements to only 5,000 steps per day or fewer (around 2.5 miles). During the first week he experienced mood swings, lethargy and headaches, all of which were alleviated by eating a McDonald's meal. As a result, Spurlock was described as being addicted. After three weeks he had heart palpitations, and was informed by his clinician that continuing with the programme could put his life at serious risk. He continued regardless and survived, but by the end of the month had gained over 11 kg and was in significantly worse mental and physical shape compared with one month previously.

This is an extreme example to make a point: our lifestyle, diet and levels of exercise have an impact on our susceptibility to disease. Exercise, good diet and rest may well boost our immune system and increase energy levels, but a lack of exercise, poor diet and insufficient sleep could shorten our concentration span, shorten our lifespan, and increase the likelihood of illness. More than that, some of our most deadly diseases are clearly linked to lifestyle. For example, the link between smoking and lung cancer is well established, as is the link between excessive alcohol consumption and liver damage. In short, God has enabled people to be part of the solution to sickness not only as we care for others, but also as we care for our own bodies and make sensible lifestyle choices.

So Christians believe that disease and sickness are not simply the way the world is, but rather a physical consequence of the brokenness between people and God. In general, they are not personal punishment. They impact on everyone in one way or another. People have a role to play in alleviating suffering through medicine and technology, and preventing it through lifestyle. For the atheist, human beings are the sole solution to the problem, because there is no-one else to help. For the theist, God in his compassion for people is in the business of mending, treating and remedying our physical brokenness. He involves doctors, engineers and research scientists in his work. Far from being anti-science or anti-progress, God is the very Being who makes them possible. This then raises the question: In what way(s) might you be part of the solution to suffering, either to your own or someone else's?

What about natural disasters?

Why does God allow natural disasters, events so much bigger than us, to occur? There are a number of different explanations to account for natural catastrophes such as earthquakes, hurricanes and tsunamis. I have summarized three below.

1. Cataclysmic events sustain the planet
The most common view held by geophysicists is that the physical mechanisms behind natural disasters are needed to sustain and create life, and have contributed to much of the natural beauty

that we enjoy. Mountain ranges and ocean trenches are formed by the riding up and forcing down of tectonic plates against one another, over time.[5] Tectonic plate movement enables nutrients from the ocean floors and beneath the earth's crust to be recycled back into the biosphere.[6] Some cosmologists hold that this mechanism is so vital that it accounts for why planet earth is unique in possessing water and sustaining life.[7] Volcanoes provide channels through which excess pressure and gases beneath the earth's crust can be released back into the atmosphere. Volcanic ash releases minerals, producing fertile soil that is valuable in agriculture. Molten lava, once cooled, allows new terrain to form. Land masses such as the Hawaiian islands were formed this way. Flooding can also be beneficial because the influx of water brings with it valuable nutrients, meaning that flood plains often yield very fertile soil once they have drained.

So natural 'disasters' are viewed by some as also having a sustaining role. They only become 'disasters' when accompanied by a loss of life. Yet the extent to which they occur on earth seems to be within boundaries, so that life is possible. Other planets such as Venus possess hundreds of volcanoes, and volcanic plains cover 80–85% of its surface.[8–10] Neptune and Jupiter have storms that make ours look tiny by comparison and call for a redefinition of the term 'extreme weather'. On earth the most powerful hurricane, a category 5, may reach 249 kph, whereas on the gaseous planet of Jupiter they may be as strong as 400 kph.[11] Jupiter is most famous for its Great Red Spot, an anticyclone 20,000 kilometres long and 12,000 wide, larger than two earths put together, with an average temperature of $-163\,°C$. This storm is so large that it consumes smaller storms and has been around for at least 400 years. On Venus and Jupiter, and every other planet we know of, life is untenable.

Britain is well known for its variable weather. We take umbrellas everywhere, even in glorious sunshine, just in case it rains. I have even been known to take one to the desert, much to the amusement of my hosts. Because of its variety, the British weather is a popular topic of conversation. We are quick to bemoan the conditions, whatever they are, be they too wet, too dry, too hot, too cold, too sunny, too cloudy. And yet, when we consider the planets around us, our weather conditions and temperature lie within such narrow limits that it is amazing that we survive at all.

Many philosophers refer to the laws of the universe as being incredibly finely tuned or intricately balanced to enable complex life.[12–14] If any of these constants of nature had changed during the first moments of the Big Bang, life in the universe would have been untenable. For example, if the gravitational force or electromagnetic force changed by as little as 1 part in 10^{40}, stars such as our sun would not have existed, rendering life impossible. Hugh Ross highlights the level of accuracy involved:

> Cover America with coins in a column reaching to the moon (380,000 km or 236,000 miles away), then do the same for a billion other continents of the same size. Paint one coin red and put it somewhere in one of the billion piles. Blindfold a friend and ask her to pick it out. The odds are about 1 in 10^{40} that she will.[15]

Even though planet earth contains cataclysmic events that can claim lives, given these ratios it is a wonder that life exists at all.

2. Nature is broken

Another viewpoint is that the earth was originally created without the capacity or need for 'natural disasters'. It was self-sustaining and beautiful but also stable. The human decision to turn away from God impacted the whole of nature and introduced volcanic activity, tectonic plate movement, hurricanes and tornadoes. Certain Bible verses describe the natural world as groaning, being subject to frustration and bondage, and decaying (Romans 8:20–22). In other words, the natural world is not as it should be because of the estrangement of people from their

Maker. Cataclysmic events serve as reminders that nature is broken because of human rebellion.

3. We are disconnected from nature

A further possibility is that it is not nature that is broken, but our connectedness with it. Those first humans enjoyed a closeness not just with their Creator, but also with the created world around them and all of its creatures. Humans were given the role of assigning names to birds, livestock and beasts, and must have spent a good deal of time with these creatures in the process (Genesis 2:19–20). Some people are able to smell in the air when a storm is coming. A tidal wave is usually preceded by a retreat of the sea water, leaving the beaches clear for minutes before it returns in a deluge. The tragic events in Asia in 2004 were all the more tragic when we heard accounts of people walking on the beaches after the water had retreated, oblivious to the possibility that it might return. Animals often have a greater awareness of natural signs than people. For example, before a tsunami cattle run to high ground, and birds go quiet before a storm. Perhaps when humans enjoyed an unhindered closeness to God they also enjoyed a heightened awareness of the natural world with all of its signs. In contrast, after turning from God, that closeness to nature was also broken or at least muddied.

The impact of poverty

A role for natural disasters in sustaining the planet seems all very well, but innocent people's lives are caught up in these mechanisms, often in their thousands. Why do so many people die in them?

Part of the answer, once again, lies in human choice. We have chosen to build densely populated cities, such as San Francisco, along fault lines. The ancient city of Pompeii was situated at the foot of a volcano. These locations bring an element of risk and increase the likelihood that large numbers of people will be injured and killed if the fault lines move or volcanoes erupt.

Injustice raises the death toll even further. The number of deaths from disasters in developing countries is generally much higher than in developed countries. The death toll in Asia after the tsunami in 2004, for example, was in the hundreds of thousands because many were living in poverty in makeshift houses close to the beaches. Landslides caused by extreme weather kill far more people in developing countries than developed ones because of the lack of infrastructure and abundance of high-density housing. Although people are generally not responsible for the event itself, human decisions, poverty and injustice undoubtedly add to the death toll.

The impact of lifestyle

During the twentieth century the earth's global temperature increased notably, and whether this was due to natural fluctuations or permanent change is an area of current debate. This increase has caused polar ice-caps to melt, leading to a global rise in sea levels. It may also have caused changes in local weather patterns, leading to, for example, increased numbers of hurricanes and tornadoes, severe flooding and landslides.[16, 17] There are many competing explanations for these changes, one of which is the impact of human lifestyle. Interestingly, in the biblical account God uniquely entrusted people with the care of the environment in which they lived: plants, animals, everything. It was a privileged position, but one that brought with it responsibility. Before we point the finger at God, consider this question: How am I using the natural resources at my disposal? Responsibly or carelessly? Sparingly or exploitatively? With concern or indifference? We are obviously not responsible for the onset of natural disasters, but our choices could have an impact upon their frequency and severity.

My problems are irrelevant?

'There's always somebody worse off than you.' Sometimes, when we are struggling, we comfort ourselves with the thought that there is always someone else going through a worse problem. This may be true, and sometimes the horrendous suffering of others does put our own situation into perspective. But this does not mean that our problems are irrelevant. Nor does it mean that God is not interested.

We assume that if many people are suffering all at the same time, as is the case after a natural disaster, then the suffering is much greater than that of just one person. On one level it is true that if every family in a village has lost loved ones, then the effect on that community is immense. And if while grieving you also have to cope with the fact of losing your home, livelihood, possessions and clean water supply, as well as famine and disease, then this would certainly be traumatic. For many in these situations, the suffering, which continues long after the media have retreated, is more than they can bear. But on another level, mass suffering can sometimes lead a person to feel that his or her individual suffering is insignificant by comparison: 'God, in his spiritual Accident & Emergency [emergency room] must have his hands full with the victims of large-scale disasters, and therefore why trouble him with my individual case!?'

My father-in-law recently lost his battle with cancer, and we entered the rollercoaster of grief. That overwhelming sense of loss and injustice at being robbed of a life led inevitably to the screaming reality that 'this is not the way things were supposed to be!' Anyone who has experienced the death of a loved one will know that death is an aberration, no matter how many people are involved. Grief remains an all-consuming, draining and powerful emotion, whether it is one person who has died or 100,000. I recall a friend describing how her friend's mother had died just before the September 11th attacks in 2001. Amid the tragedy of 9/11 this friend had said, 'I don't know what all the fuss is about. Do people not realize that my mother has just died?' Suffering is very personal, and the suffering of the one is just as valid and important as the suffering of the many.

You matter to God

Whether you are alone and grieving your last living relative, or you are in a refugee camp and surrounded by suffering at every turn, you matter to God. Your suffering matters to God. It grieves him. When you suffer, he suffers with you, and therefore no problem is too small or too big for him. The God we meet in the Bible is a God to whom all people matter, and who says, 'Come to me, ALL you who are weary and burdened, and I will give you rest' (Matthew 11:28; capitals mine). Unlike a junior doctor in A&E on a Saturday night, he will not grow tired or weary. His capacity to love hurting people is limitless.

Rachel's story

I have had multiple sclerosis since I was twenty-eight, and I describe things in terms of 'life before MS' and 'life since MS'.
I used to have a huge amount of energy to accomplish things. We had a dog, and I used to enjoy long walks with family and friends. I also loved swimming regularly. My motto was: 'Work until the job is done.' This could mean long work hours, painting the house or accomplishing something as a hobby. My husband and I also travelled quite a bit together, and I really enjoyed that.

In autumn 2001 I noticed a numb patch on my leg, and found that after cycling I couldn't make out the details of people's faces or where the contours were in the road. I remember saying to my mum, 'There is something wrong with me, but I don't know what it is.' That winter, my husband and I were working in Latvia, and I noticed that everything seemed sepia-coloured. I came home, went to the doctor and began a series of tests and scans. Finally, in May 2002, I was diagnosed as having MS. At the time all I felt was huge relief that it wasn't a tumour and that I didn't have to have brain surgery! And since I felt fine, it didn't really seem to be real. The hardest thing to hear was that there is no cure for MS, only prevention and treatment. I was told to rest a lot, stay healthy and think about drug therapy.

Almost immediately I changed from full-time work to part-time work, to balance activity and rest. Two years later, my husband had a sabbatical, and I joined him in the USA, where we went skiing and ice-skating and generally adventuring. Everything was normal. We decided to try for a baby, and when she was born in 2005 I felt incredibly fit and well. In many ways MS was an invisible disease, only occasionally interrupting life when I became fatigued.

When our daughter was three I caught flu, and afterwards had a serious relapse that resulted in a decline in my walking and a decision to get a walking stick. This was a hard adjustment psychologically, as people treated me differently with a stick, albeit often with the best intentions. Being cared for doesn't come easily to me!

With MS there is a bucket of energy and ability that can either be emptied slowly or all at once. The picture I often use is of a bank. I deposit rest and withdraw activity, but there is no overdraft facility. When the bank is empty, it's empty. I remember one day when I tried to overdraw. After much pleading from my daughter, we agreed to cycle home from school together. Normally I would have driven, because it is too far to walk. As I got near the school to collect her I realized that my legs weren't pushing the pedals any more. I got off the bike to cross the road, and my legs just wouldn't move. I had to put my bike against a wall, sit down on the pavement, pull out my phone and call my parents.

I experienced such a mix of emotions: humiliation at having to sit on the pavement unable to move; worry that we would be late in picking up my daughter and that she would wonder where I was, or that the school would think I was a bad parent; resignation (I'll never cycle again) and fury (how dare MS attack me). Mum came to take my daughter home, which was very exciting for a five-year-old. I left my bike, and it was eventually stolen – but as I don't ride any more I just hope that the person who took it will use it more than I can! I am reminded regularly of my limits. I can no longer work until the job is done, and that frustrates me.

Some people might say that my faith is just a psychological crutch to keep me going through a difficult illness. I would say I had faith in Jesus long before MS, since I was four, in fact. I have Christian parents, attended church as a child and became a Christian one evening along with my favourite babysitter, Margery. We were reading the story of Zacchaeus. I remember thinking that here was a naughty man, but that Jesus wanted to be his friend anyway. That Jesus could be my friend, even though I knew I had been quite naughty, really made an impression on me.

So we prayed and I said, 'Dear Lord Jesus, please come into my heart and be my friend. Amen.'

Margery said, 'Do you know what that means?'

And I said, 'I'm a Christian.'

This event is a 'photograph' in my head of the beginning of my own journey. Since then my faith has become more sophisticated and been challenged, but the grounding is still that Jesus is my friend.

My faith now isn't based on God doing nice things for me, but on the evidence that compels me. The truth that Jesus is my friend has since been backed up by experiential and biblical evidence so compelling that this is what sustains me. There are times, if I'm really honest, when emotionally it's not pleasant, and I would much rather be able to rage at God and say, 'I'm done with you.' But where else would I go? This isn't a crutch, because it's more powerful, more robust and more permanent than a crutch could ever be. It is true, even when I would rather it was not true.

I don't think that God is punishing me or that my MS is somehow my fault. If God is capricious and just loses his temper and does nasty things, then the idea of punishment would make sense, but the God we see in the Bible is slow to get angry, immensely loving, trustworthy and also unchanging. But I do think that my sin contributes in general to a broken world. I remember the story of the Editor of *The Times* posting a question: 'What's wrong with the world?' And G. K. Chesterton wrote in, 'Sir, what's wrong with the world? I am!'

Since my diagnosis I have come to see God as somebody who grieves with me over my disability. This was something I'd always known about God, but through MS I have experienced it much more deeply. My own dad has helped me understand what it means that God is 'Father'. Dad took the news of my MS deeply, but then also connected with me deeply on it. He gave me space to struggle with it.

God, like my dad, is not unemotional about my suffering, but in fact has the awful job of watching me go through something that was never part of his design for the world. He doesn't fold his arms and stand back from me. He comes into my struggles and works through them. Through MS and through other people, I have experienced God's love in a different way. God's love is more than a cosmic: 'I love the world and everyone in it.' It's intimate: 'I love you and have deep personal concern for you, Rachel.' I experience a strong peace at times when I should be fearful, and also very practical provisions of help and care when I most need them.

MS is part of my story, but it is not the end of my story.

MS is part of my story, but it is not the end of my story. One of the writers in the Bible, Paul, says, 'Though outwardly we are wasting away, yet inwardly we are being renewed day by day' (2 Corinthians 4:16). That's what eternal life looks like for me. There is an inner change that means that God is with me now. It's not something I have to wait for until I die. Eternal life began when I was four, and because of that God lives with me right now, changing me and changing the way I see and do life. I've personally struggled with panic, and sometimes there have been evenings when everything has looked very bleak. At the same time God has given me enormous joy in the moment because this is not all there is. Outwardly I may well fade away quite significantly, but I don't have to disappear because I'm being made new every day that I walk with God.

My daughter, who loves activity and sport, asks me frequently, 'When will you be able to run, Mummy?'

I am very honest and say, 'I won't be able to run now. But when we meet Jesus, when I see him face to face, then absolutely without question, I'll be able to run.'

This isn't wishful thinking. I base it on the promise that everything will be made new, that my body will be made new. I will be able to run, and I'm really looking forward to it.

8 Can a broken story be fixed?

It is nearly Christmas time. The lights are twinkling, the songs and carols are being dusted off for yet another year, and the shops are as chaotic as ever. As I wander around the stores I am always drawn to the number of autobiographies that are released in late November. Publishers are obviously shrewd to release books at the same time as people are delving especially deeply into their wallets. Yet this flurry of publishing perhaps reflects something deeper. We are drawn to real stories. Yes, science fiction and novels have their place, but there is undoubtedly a huge interest in people recounting real events. A Google search of the words 'my story' alone yields over 140 million hits. We love to tell our story and we love to hear them from other people.

There was a time when autobiographies would have been written only by those who had made a significant contribution to society and had a legacy to leave. Authors were usually well on in years, enabling a broader perspective over their whole life. Former political leaders such as Margaret Thatcher, Nelson Mandela and Winston Churchill come to mind. Today anybody can publish 'their story'. Our stories can even be viewed through countless blogs or YouTube movies. In our celebrity culture people rise and fall in and out of fame at a rapid rate, and therefore autobiographies are published at the peak of fame, for who knows how long it will last? We are inundated with offers from celebrities to tell us 'their story', offered a window into their lives, into their struggles and triumphs, successes and regrets.

In this book we have journeyed with five individuals through their stories. Some people's suffering has reached a resolution, but for others the struggle is ongoing with no prospect of relenting. Yes, there is strength to cope and comfort in grief, but as for 'why?' or 'why me?', there are no clear answers. For many the grief will remain raw for years to come; for some it may even become worse. Some will learn to live with tragedy, but never overcome it. Our stories are broken. Is there any hope of relief? Is there any way that they can be fixed, or is that just a pipe dream?

Is there a bigger story?

In order to answer this question we need to ask another question: Is there a bigger overarching story, a bigger picture or meta-narrative into which all our individual stories fit? Interestingly, many of the biographies offered to us are written by people in their twenties or even their teens. The Canadian pop artist Justin Bieber published his biography, *First Step 2 Forever: My Story*, in 2010 at the age of just sixteen. Intriguing though his rise to fame may be, isn't the story of a teenager only just beginning? Could it be that there is a bigger and richer perspective to be gained by having lived across several decades and generations, giving greater significance to the events of our lives? And if this is true of biographies, then could it also be relevant to how we view suffering?

Individual stories

Today in the West there is a resistance to the idea of overarching stories. The possibility of there being a bigger perspective to life is viewed with suspicion, and those advocating it can be viewed as arrogant or as trying to control others. History, the contrary argument goes, is comprised of individual stories, each with some subjective meaning, but with no ultimate meaning or relationship to one another. People may invent a bigger picture in order to bring comfort and give greater meaning to their life, but this grand perspective simply does not exist.

If this is the case, then can a broken story be fixed? It depends on what you mean. You can relieve some of the brokenness through relationships and through striving for justice. But there is no ultimate reason why you have suffered like this, and so trying to find one is futile. The late Christopher Hitchens, a bestselling author, polemicist and atheist, was interviewed in 2011 on CNN about the news of his diagnosis of terminal oesophageal cancer. He was asked whether, despite his atheism, he had been tempted to ask the question: 'Why me?'

He responded, 'You can't avoid the question, however stoic you are. You can only bat it away as a silly one. Millions of people die every day. Everyone's got to go sometime.'[1]

In other words, one must make the most of the human capacity to relieve suffering and then face it head-on. Genetics has seen to it that your story is one of billions and billions. It has significance to you, but eventually it and you will be swept away as evolution continues on its path.

There is a glaring inconsistency here with the view that there are no overarching stories. The person making the observation assumes that they are somehow outside of these individual stories, looking in. In other words, they must somehow have a bird's-eye view of all individual stories in order to reach the conclusion that there are no overarching stories. That is, they are proposing the overarching story that there are no overarching stories! It seems that the question of whether or not there is a big picture to life is inescapable. Every religion offers one, atheism included, and many people seem to desire one, so perhaps a better question to be asking is: 'Which one is correct?'

Repeating stories

As we saw in previous chapters, Eastern thought holds that after death humans are reincarnated because their soul lives on and attaches to another body. But the struggles of this life are carried over from past lives and will also impact future ones. Can a broken story be fixed according to Eastern thought? No. The fixing takes place in the next life and beyond, but it will not be *your* story as such. You can only hope to begin another story in another body as another being, and hope that your deeds in this life will see to it that you return again as a human and not an animal, vegetable or mineral.

One great story

In Christianity, life is not repeating itself, nor is it a chaotic jumble of meaningless events, but instead it is projecting forwards towards a goal. The world that we see around us was started by God, is upheld by God, and one day will be completed by God. Humans are created uniquely by God and are unspeakably precious. They are born once, live once, die once and are asked to justify their lives to God and face an eternal destiny based on the decisions they made about Jesus Christ. In other words, God is the start and finish of every story.

The world that we see around us was started by God, is upheld by God, and one day will be completed by God.

In a book or play it is the role of the author to tell the story. If that book is then made into a film or TV series, the author may contribute ideas and vision. Occasionally the author may feature in the production, and in so doing offer a unique translation of written words into real life. This is Christianity. Jesus Christ stepped inside the story of human history that he authored. He defeated the ultimate enemy, the ultimate aberration, the only certainty that all people face: death, and with it evil. Here is the crucial point. Death has been defeated, but not yet *removed*. Jesus intervened in the middle of the story, not the end. We are living at a time in history in which the defeat of evil and death happened in the past, but we are still waiting for them to be fully removed in the future. Yet the Bible is clear that a future age or era will come in which evil and death will be utterly banished and God will be fully seen. The very end of the Bible (Revelation 21:3–4) gives us a glimpse of this time to come:

> And I heard a loud voice from the throne saying, 'Look! God's dwelling-place is now among the people, and he will dwell with them. They will be his people, and God himself will be with them and be their God. "He will wipe every tear from their eyes. There will be no more death" or mourning or crying or pain, for the old order of things has passed away.'

This time to come will be in a real place, free from evil, but also a place in which God will be fully present. At the moment we catch glimpses of God and of that freedom, but then we will see him face to face. Because of him the chains will come off and we will be free to be ourselves. We will be free to do what we are ultimately made to do: worship God free from fear of death, because death will be gone. The sufferings we have endured and have watched others go through will be seen in a new light. They will still matter and may not be completely forgotten, because even Jesus' resurrected body had visible scars from his crucifixion, but the joy of seeing God face to face will make everything new. Rachel will be free of MS and able to run.

So according to Christianity, can a broken story be fixed? It can, by embedding it into a much bigger story in which evil has been defeated and will one day be removed, in which good will ultimately triumph, justice will ultimately be done and suffering will ultimately and permanently end. Because of Jesus Christ there is reason for much hope, even in the midst of tragedy.

C. S. Lewis puts it well, at the very end of his Chronicles of Narnia series:

> The term is over: the holidays have begun. The dream is ended: this is the morning . . . And for us this is the end of all the stories . . . But for them it was only the beginning of the real story. All their life in this world and all their adventures in Narnia had only been the cover and the title page: now at last they were beginning Chapter One of the Great Story which no one on earth has read: which goes on for ever: in which every chapter is better than the one before.[2]

Why doesn't God just get rid of evil once and for all?

For some the mere mention of a new age or era makes Christianity seem excessive. Indeed a prevalent belief is that the world we can see and touch is all there is. Isn't the suggestion of anything 'other' surely within a realm reserved for religious eccentrics? At the same time there is a fascination with apocalyptic events. Our movies such as *The Day after Tomorrow*, *2012* and *War of the Worlds* are full of interpretations of the end of the world. People frequently ask, 'If God is so powerful and is able to defeat evil, then why doesn't he just get rid of it once and for all?' In order to answer this question we must at least be willing to consider the possibility of a new era.

God does indeed intend to remove evil completely. He is not happy to watch his world suffer forever, and he fully intends to remove evil. But why doesn't he do it *today*? The short answer is because today not everyone would make it. If God were to remove every trace of evil from our world today, then yes, the torturers and mass murderers and child abusers would be stopped in their tracks, but then so too would you and I. Our definition of evil differs greatly from God's. Our definition refers to evil in those who make life unpalatable for us. God's definition encompasses everything that pours out of a heart set on living without him. Therefore evil encompasses not only actions but also attitudes such as envy, jealousy and greed, and speech such as insult and gossip. Evil pervades both the visible and invisible. It is both secret and public. Put in these terms, if God were to remove evil today, would anyone at all survive?

On our own merit the answer is no, but there is one person who has made it possible for us to continue standing before God when that day comes: Jesus Christ. It is one thing to write your own story and market it. It is quite another for someone else to think your life significant enough to write it down on your behalf. Four ordinary men: a fisherman, a taxman, a congregation member and a doctor were sufficiently stunned by Jesus' life, death and resurrection that they each carefully wrote down his story, producing the four Gospel accounts we have today. What did this man accomplish that made him so appealing? He defeated evil and death by taking them to the grave with him and leaving them there before rising again. He did this on a cosmic scale, but to have any impact it needs to be taken up by us as individuals. On the day when God removes evil once and for all, those who trust and believe that Jesus has done this for them will not be condemned.

A perfect world

As a child, before I even knew God, I used to draw pictures of perfect towns with cute houses and tidily cut grass and children with neatly brushed hair who were kind to one another. This may be the outworking of a perfectionist personality, but could it also be that before I knew God he knew me, and had placed a desire in me even at a young age for a place in which things would be set right? Our movies are also full of the desire for utopia and the aspiration to end violence and establish peace and justice. The Bible is clear that this longing has been put in every human heart by the God who made us. In other words, God has 'set eternity in the human heart; yet no one can fathom what God has done from beginning to end' (Ecclesiastes 3:11).

Such a place will exist, and we are designed to be part of it, but there is a disclaimer. We are not *guaranteed* to be part of it. The human heart has a longing for eternity, but also a propensity for evil. To engage with eternity we need to deal with evil first, through Jesus. If we do, then our hopes and dreams of an idyllic world will be fulfilled on the day that God removes evil once and for all, but if we do not, then we will be part of the evil that is removed. In fact, that day will be the worst one imaginable.

Many think that the reason God has not yet removed evil is because he is indifferent to our suffering. In reality, it is the opposite. God has not yet removed evil once and for all precisely *because* he cares deeply about people. His desire is that every person would be included in this final era without evil, and he withholds its arrival to allow still more people the opportunity to follow Jesus and therefore be included.

What is heaven?

There is a global fascination with the paranormal. The tourist industry in every major city offers books and tours that recount stories of ghostly appearances and unusual happenings. A common view is that the heaven that Christians refer to is simply a place in which such beings are more populous. That is, the existence that awaits Christians is a woolly, ghostly existence inferior to our current one. The Bible gives us a very different picture. This future era will not be filled with ghostly vacuous beings floating around in some kind of limbo state. It will consist of real people, living in a real place with real bodies, made new because they have been resurrected to new life. In fact, the Bible does not refer to heaven alone, but to 'a new heaven and a new earth' (Revelation 21:1). This new heaven and earth will be not only as real as the world we see and touch today, but even more real, even more vibrant, even more alive.

Reincarnation or resurrection?

After the death of Princess Diana in 1997 there was a huge out-pouring of grief across Britain. The scale of mourning was unprecedented, and many left flowers and messages either in London or in their home towns. The theologian Tom Wright points out that the types of messages revealed a variety of views about what happens beyond death: 'One message left in London spoke as in the Princess's own voice: "I did not leave you at all. I am still with you. I am in the sun and in the wind. I am even in the rain. I did not die. I am with you all."'[3] Such a view permeates Western thought today, but has its roots in the Eastern concept of rebirth or reincarnation. Rebirth sounds very appealing and not dissimilar to the Christian message. But are rebirth and new birth, or reincarnation and resurrection, just different ways of saying the same thing?

In short, they could not be more different. Reincarnation refers to rebirth into a new but mortal body that is not neces-sarily human. Moreover, each reincarnation, though progressing towards perfection, is an intermediate state into which one could be reborn an indefinite number of times. In fact, there is no guarantee of escaping the birth-death cycle at all. As Ravi Zacharias puts it: 'If life is cyclical and there is no beginning to the incarnations, why is there an end?'[4] Perhaps some are drawn to reincarnation because it is more palatable than the idea of hell in Christianity. But is a lengthy cycle of death and rebirth for which there is no guarantee of escape a better alternative?

In contrast, resurrection does not refer to life after death. In the words of Tom Wright, 'it is the reversal of death itself.'[5] It is guaranteed for those who believe and trust that Jesus' resur-rection has made ours possible. We are not resurrected into a different body as a different person or creature, but rather our current body will be made new. We ourselves will be made new.

People will not be blended into one uniform state. God has created each person uniquely, and it is culture, peer pressure and sin that force people into a mould into which they don't fit. Our bodily resurrection reverses misplaced identity, and preserves and even magnifies our true individual identity, because the binding effects of sin will be gone. Rachel will be free from MS and able to run, but she will always still be Rachel.

Eternal life

For a Buddhist or Hindu, rebirth begins when you die. Many assume that the same applies to Christianity. That is, Christians believe in life after death, and to become a Christian is to gain a ticket to an afterworld to which we are admitted beyond the grave. There is even better news than this. New birth starts in this life, because the forerunner of new birth broke through to earth 2,000 years ago in the person of Jesus Christ and made it possible for us to be born again now. In other words, we can start over and have our spirit reawakened by God's Spirit, the Holy Spirit. The impact of this is so dramatic that Jesus likens it to the birth of a new person. Our thoughts, speech, lifestyle, attitudes, work and relationships are transformed for the better. We will enter the new age fully in the future, but new birth can be ours now.

When God broke into human life as Jesus he brought with him this future era, referred to as the 'kingdom of God', super-imposing it onto a mundane earthly existence. This breaking in of the kingdom of God is the source of all the miracles reported in the Gospel accounts, such as people being healed of diseases and sickness, raised from the dead and freed from demon possession. We see a glimpse of this future era. Even though Jesus has now returned to heaven, his kingdom remains, so that there are two dimensions to life even today: the kingdom of God and the kingdom of earth. Christian hope is about seeing God's plans and purposes brought to bear upon daily life in a world in which evil has been defeated but not yet removed. This is what Jesus meant when he instructed us to pray:

Your kingdom come,
your will be done,
    on earth as it is in heaven.
(Matthew 6:10)

We may have uttered these words reluctantly in chapel or Sunday school when growing up, without realizing what they meant. If they were truly meant and lived out, then most of the problems on our planet would disappear overnight.

Eternal life is not something done to you when you die. Jesus Christ himself embodied eternal life and defined it in the hours before he died. He said, 'Now this is eternal life: that [people] may know you, the only true God, and Jesus Christ, whom you have sent' (John 17:3 NIV 1984). In other words, eternal life is a relationship with the only true God, Jesus, who is alive and relevant today. Eternal life begins the moment we choose to follow Jesus, when he awakens us from a state of spiritual slumber or even death. Eternal life begins this side of the grave, continues into eternity and is on offer to everyone. Today.

Our stories in this life are broken. Yet there is hope. There is a bigger story that wraps around all of our individual stories, in which good will triumph, evil will be destroyed, justice will be done and we will be able to see God clearly. We will enter this fully in the future, but can encounter it now in part. Becoming a Christian is about connecting our own story into the story of Jesus Christ and seeing God's kingdom break into our own life. But it is something we have to choose. This is the subject of our next chapter: 'How do I move forward from here?'

9 How do I move forward from here?

Conrad and I became Christians as adults. We did not know each other at the time, but shared very similar perceptions of what Christians were supposed to be like. It went something like this. Religion is for the needy. Christians are people who lack social graces, a sense of humour, fashion sense and emotional intelligence. Church is a kind of club or gathering point for all such people who, having failed to connect with 'normal' people, resort to just meeting with their own kind: others of similar social awkwardness. My husband clearly remembers his first contact with Christians at university. He was surprised by how 'normal' they were. Quite unexpectedly, he began to meet people he could relate to. His perception of Christians was being challenged, and this was the beginning of a journey for him.

This chapter is about putting theory into practice. It differs from all the rest, because everything so far has been theory or other people's stories, whereas this chapter deals with application. It deals with *your* story, since finding answers to suffering is not just an intellectual exercise. If God is real, if Jesus really did die and rise again, then there is hope for the future and comfort in the present, for all.

Is my suffering happening for a reason?

Sometimes people try to make sense of their suffering by finding reasons for it. 'Things happen for a reason' is a common expression, but this can seem overly formulaic. I well remember times when the reasons for my own suffering were forced upon me before I was ready, as though by answering this question a solution was provided and my troubles were over. I also recall times when in my zeal I did the same thing to others. I too have been eager to find a reason, without stopping first to sit with my friend and enter into his or her pain. The question of purpose in pain is very often one to which the 'worried well' run, but from which the sufferer bolts. It seems like a good idea in theory, but when in the midst of the storm the biggest desire is that the pain be taken away. As Philip Yancey and Paul Brand titled their book: *Pain: The Gift Nobody Wants*.

Is my suffering happening for a reason? When a mother's children are swept away before her very eyes by a tsunami, is there a purpose, a reason for her agony? Is there something she needs to learn? When tens of thousands die in an earthquake, is there a purpose? When an elderly person is neglected and bereft of dignity in a retirement home, is there a purpose? Sometimes the only reason that can be given is that humanity as a whole is out of kilter with its Maker and everyone is dragged along.

Many can speak of a time of suffering that deepened their character, or deepened a relationship, or caused them to view life in a new way. Yes, God can certainly bring good out of suffering, but that does not necessarily mean that the good is the *reason* why the suffering happened in the first place. Sometimes the only reason that can be given is that people have forgotten and neglected their ultimate purpose, which is to know and follow God, and everybody is affected.

So God does seem to use suffering to reconnect people into their ultimate purpose: relationship with him. When life is good we can feel like we are invincible, and sometimes it is only in the place of suffering that God and our need for him can be clearly seen. For Will, personal tragedy was the beginning of a journey back to God. Could it be that God is trying to attract your attention through your suffering?

Could it be that God is trying to attract your attention through your suffering?

It's not that you are being singled out as needing God any more than the next person, but just as the disconnect from God impacts on everyone, so the opportunity to reconnect to God is available to all, including you.

I've tried praying, so why did nothing happen?

According to a recent MORI poll survey,[1] 63% of people admit to having prayed at some point in their life. Perhaps we remember bedside prayers as children or saying grace at the dining table. Or perhaps we think of a confessional booth and the associated guilt. Or perhaps we have talked to the four walls about a loved one, hoping that someone will hear. Our experiences of prayer are varied. Some have tried it, been disappointed by it, and concluded that it simply doesn't work.

If God is trying to attract our attention and wants to make himself known, then why doesn't he just answer our prayers? Once again there are no simple answers. Sometimes the reasons relate to God and sometimes they relate to us. Sometimes we ask for things that are not good for us or other people, and so God says, 'no'. Sometimes we haven't prayed in such a way that a clear answer can be given. If we pray, 'God, please help me to get through this day. I'm feeling really ill', God may well answer, but it's often our tendency to put it down to coincidence. It was the medicine, the strong coffee, and we were probably about to get better anyway. My experience is that God responds to very specific prayers. In fact, the more specific, the better.

Some have found it helpful to keep a diary of the things they have asked God about, and this has been evidence enough to start believing. As a scientist, I like to think of answered prayer in terms of data points on a graph. When I became a Christian I had very little data and remember early on having some unmistakable answers to prayer that encouraged me to keep asking and adding more data points. But even so, the first few could still have been put down to coincidence. Fifteen years later I now have thousands and thousands of data points, and any rigorous scientist would allow the data to speak for itself. So are there things, big or small, for which you've tried everything else except asking God? In the words of former Archbishop of Canterbury, William Temple, 'When I pray, coincidences happen, and when I don't, they don't.'

We read in Philippians 4:6–7 (NIV 1984): 'Do not be anxious about anything, but in everything, by prayer and petition, with thanksgiving, present your requests to God. And the peace of God, which transcends all understanding, will guard your hearts and your minds in Christ Jesus.'

Why some prayers are answered with 'yes' and others with 'no' or 'not yet' is not always understandable. Yet there is a transaction that is guaranteed. If you deposit prayer in the God bank, you will withdraw peace. Peace that stands guard over emotions and thoughts, bringing protection from panic. Peace even when everyone else at work is stressed. Peace at 2am when your teenager has not returned from a party. Peace when your very life is in danger.

Forgiving others

Another reason why prayers may feel like they are not being answered is because we are withholding forgiveness, holding a grudge against people who have wronged us. This too can drive a wedge between us and God, blocking our prayer life. Forgiveness is central to a healthy relationship with God, because our reluctance to forgive stems from not having understood and received the depth of his forgiveness extended to us.

Perhaps people picture a stern God who demands that we repent and ask his forgiveness, because until we do he cannot love us. In fact, love is first. Love is what makes forgiveness necessary. The way I relate to my own children helps me to understand this. I remember hearing the heartbeat of my children before I could see them, and I well remember them being handed to me in the first moments of their life. Was their need of my forgiveness on my mind? I think not. It couldn't have been further away. They were precious and loved. Forgiveness was necessary later (most parents agree that this is around the age of two!), but only so that love could be upheld. Forgiveness was needed to deal with their waywardness, so that they could continue to enjoy my love.

Similarly, God is not repentance. God is not forgiveness. God is love. Love comes first. Forgiveness enables love gone wrong to be restored. God secured our forgiveness by sending Jesus to absorb our waywardness on the cross and take it with him to death. He was cut off from the Father's love, so that we could become free to enjoy God's love again. We are offered forgiveness. A clean start, a new beginning, not having our past mistakes held against us. The question is: will we ask for and accept this forgiveness? The answer impacts on everything, including our ability to forgive others.

Isn't forgiveness for the weak?

Britain's inner-city streets have become notorious for their knife crime. This fact became all too real for Gee Verona Walker whose son Anthony Walker was murdered on Merseyside in 2005 in a racially motivated attack. Two men were convicted of Anthony's murder, and yet at the trial Mrs Walker extended forgiveness to these same men. Her words outside the court were: 'Do I forgive them? At the point of death Jesus said, "I forgive them because they don't know what they did." I've got to forgive them. I still forgive them. My family and I still stand by what we believe: forgiveness.'[2]

Forgiveness seems to provoke a variety of different responses. In some people it's admiration that a person would find such goodness in their heart towards their offender. In others it's outrage, because forgiving someone is seen as taking the easy way out. People who forgive have failed to face grim reality and are hiding their grief behind religious behaviour. Forgiveness doesn't work. It is impossible, a cop-out, a pipe dream.

It is important that we understand what forgiveness is not. Firstly, forgiveness does not mean that the crime against you no longer matters. It matters immensely. Secondly, forgiveness does not necessarily involve reconciliation. We can forgive people who have already died for example. Thirdly, forgiveness does not mean that the offender is excused. Gee Verona clearly forgave the men who killed Anthony, but at their trial she also attested to their guilt and need for imprisonment.

Christian forgiveness is about choosing to let God deal with the perpetrator. We are assured that there will be a day when God will hold all people accountable for their lives, and on that day there will be no mistakes or miscarriages of justice. Forgiveness is about choosing not to become as bitter as the people we have been hurt by. It is far from the easy option, because everything within us screams to hold on to our right to revenge. Yet unforgiveness can have a crippling effect on our thoughts, emotions, relationships, attitudes and even our physical health. It is a form of imprisonment. Tim Keller says,

> I remember once counseling a sixteen-year-old girl about the
> anger she felt towards her father. We weren't getting anywhere

until I said to her, 'Your father has defeated you, as long as you hate him. You will stay trapped in your anger unless you forgive him thoroughly from the heart and begin to love him.' Something thawed in her when she realized that. She went through the suffering of costly forgiveness, which at first feels far worse than bitterness, into eventual freedom. Forgiveness must be granted before it can be felt, but it does come eventually. It leads to a new peace, a resurrection. It is the only way to stop the spread of the evil.[3]

I frequently hear people say, 'I could never forgive that person.' Christians might actually agree, but then add a further three words, '. . . without God's help'. When God sets the incredibly high and painful standard of letting go of our bitterness and rage, he does not ask us to do it alone. Rather he gives us the resources and ability to do what we never thought was humanly possible. Forgiveness is only possible when we grasp and receive God's forgiveness and love to us through Jesus. Forgiveness is the stuff of heaven, not of earth.

Forgiveness is the stuff of heaven, not of earth.

If I become a Christian, will I suffer less?

Does becoming a Christian mean that my troubles will disappear? Well, if you have read even a couple of chapters of this book, hopefully it will be obvious by now that the answer is 'no'. Christians are subject to illness, crime and earthquakes, just the same as everyone else. And yet there is still a perception in the West that Christianity is just about making life a little better. We turn to God, and teach our children to turn to him, when we need good weather, or a particular exam result, or to make granny better, and then we question his existence when he doesn't deliver. We expect that God is there to protect and look after us at all costs, and the majority of our prayers concern these sorts of requests. Is it any surprise then that we struggle so much with the issue of suffering? Part of the reason that the 'Why me?' or 'Why?' questions are asked by the church is because of an incomplete understanding of what it means to be a Christian. Being a Christian is about putting God and his purposes above everything else, and sometimes this may mean that we suffer less, but at other times we may suffer more.

After turning to God some people have stories of a dramatic end to suffering. Others have had no noticeable change, and for some life has even got worse. I recently heard a story of a girl aged fifteen whose father threw her out of the house in the middle of the night when she would not recant her decision to follow Christ. So there is an additional suffering connected to following Jesus. Jesus was clear that we are not to be surprised by this. Shortly before he died he said, 'If the world hates you, keep in mind that it hated me first' (John 15:18), and earlier in his ministry he spoke of the need for his followers to take up their cross and follow him (Luke 9:23). In other words, some of the suffering that Jesus went through will be experienced by his followers too.

In the West this is perhaps more subtle. Christians could, for example, be sidelined in the workplace, or face disapproval from family members, or be falsely accused. In other parts of the world the suffering is more severe. Christians are frequently driven from their homes, heavily fined, denied access to work, beaten, raped, and some are even killed. Christians down the ages have also suffered and died for following Christ. In more barbaric times they were crucified, thrown to the lions, burned at the stake, sawn in two, and slow-roasted over a fire for their beliefs. There is a cost to following Jesus that we must take into consideration. 'In this world you will have trouble. But . . . ', and here is the crunch, ' . . . take heart! I have overcome the world' (John 16:33). But this is not the end of the story. We are offered extraordinary strength and comfort from God to cope with circumstances that we never believed possible. He promises to be with us wherever we are. Even on our deathbed we will not be alone, and he will lead us into even greater life with him.

Will I be less 'me' if I become a Christian?

Many people ask the above question, afraid that becoming a Christian involves receiving a lobotomy that will instantly turn them into a 'religious person', fitting into all the, often cringe-worthy, stereotypes. In fact, becoming a Christian means becoming *more* like yourself, not more like someone you are not. It is sin that tries to make us into people we are not, but God who restores us to our true selves. A disconnect from God causes the mask to go on, but a reconnect with him takes it off. A key part of Grace's story is that knowing God connects people more deeply with who they really are: 'I know who I am because I know who he is.' To many people's surprise, God is interested not just in our spirituality, but also in our humanity. It was given to us by him, and therefore when we awaken the spiritual dimension there is a parallel restoration of our humanity. We become more alive, more concerned about others, more engaged with the world we live in, more content with ourselves, more aware of what we are good at, and of what God has made us to do. We cover up less and less, and gradually become more and more authentic. Some people describe becoming a Christian as becoming fundamentally happier 'in your skin', more content with who God has made you to be.

Am I alone in this?

Becoming a Christian means becoming part of a wider body of people who also follow Christ. Jesus was clear that Christians are family, and should love and care for one another as if they were blood relatives. This is what church is, or is what it is supposed to be. It seems that one of the ways in which God cares for people when they are suffering is through other people. During Conrad's times of illness we have been loved and supported by people in all kinds of practical ways. People brought meals, prayed for and with us, and looked after our children, so that we could rest. We were never intended to live in isolation nor suffer in isolation. Very often God's comfort comes to us through other people. However far from or close to the ideal you feel you are, part of God's solution to a suffering world is the church.

How do I become a Christian?

Keble College Chapel, Oxford houses one of two copies of William Holman Hunt's oil-on-canvas painting, *The Light of the World*. The painting shows Christ standing outside a door at dawn. Large weeds suggest that the door has remained firmly shut for years, or possibly has never been opened at all. The painting is based on the following verse from the last book in the Bible: 'Here I am! I stand at the door and knock. If anyone hears my voice and opens the door, I will come in and eat with that person, and they with me' (Revelation 3:20). The voice in this verse is that of Jesus Christ, long after his resurrection. An important part of the painting is that the door has no handle on the outside. This was not an oversight, but a deliberate way of depicting the freedom of choice that people are given by God. God would love to open the door, but he never forces it open. The only way to open the door is from the inside.

The only way to open the door is from the inside.

What it looks like to 'open the door' varies between people. For some it involves a dramatic decision, for others a process taking weeks, months, even years. For some it involves praying alone at home. For others it involves finally saying yes to attending that Alpha[4] or Christianity Explored[5] course that your friend keeps mentioning. Or it may involve all of these things. The common denominator is an internal shift from 'I'm living my way' to 'I'm living God's way'.

A few years ago I helped with an Alpha course in a local prison. On one particular week we were discussing whether or not God speaks to people today. After a discussion we had a period of quiet to see if God wanted to say anything to the men. Slightly sceptical, they agreed and all became quiet. After a few minutes we asked if anything had happened. There was an awkwardness, but then one man said, 'Yeah, I heard the words, "Come dancing with me, my son."' The young man probably paid a price for his admission. No doubt there were jibes and mocking back on the wing. And yet it was apparent that those words could not have been of his own making. Such tender words from a hardened man whose life was written on his face and who had hardly danced in his life, let alone been referred to as 'son'. 'Come dancing with me, my son.' Not, 'Get on your knees and repent', nor 'You'd better be damn sorry for the trouble you've caused', but 'Come dancing with me, my son.'

The invitation extends to all. Will you dance?

We don't have all the answers on suffering, but we are offered an incredible relationship with the One who does. Whether you are in a painful or a happy place, be reconciled to the God who has always loved you, who offers you forgiveness for the past, comfort in the present and hope for the future. This is the most important decision of all. Suffering or no suffering, you will never regret it.

Notes

Frances's story

1. The link to the Radio 4 broadcast of *Remembering Millie* is
   http://www.bbc.co.uk/programmes/b01gvlg4.

1. If God exists, then why is there so much evil and suffering in the world?

1. The Council for Secular Humanism http://www.
   secularhumanism.org/index.php (accessed 13 March 2012).
2. Phil Zuckerman, 'Atheism: Contemporary Numbers and Patterns',
   in Michael Martin (ed.), *The Cambridge Companion to Atheism*
   (Cambridge University Press, 2007).
3. J. L. Mackie, 'Evil and Omnipotence', in Basil Mitchell (ed.),
   Philosophy of Religion (Oxford University Press, 1970), p. 92.
4. Ibid., p. 218.
5. Protagoras in Plato's *Theaetetus*, section 152a.
6. *Today*, BBC Radio 4 (broadcast 10 August 2011, 08:12).
7. Jeffrey A. Schaler, *Peter Singer under Fire: The Moral Iconoclast Faces
   His Critics* (Open Court Publishing, 2009), p. 162.
8. Norman L. Geisler, *Christian Ethics* (Baker Academic, 1989), p. 24.
9. Eric Michael Johnson, 'Survival of the Kindest', *Seed* magazine,
   24 September 2009.
10. Swami Prabhavananda, *Spiritual Heritage of India* (Vedanta Society
    of S. California, 1963), p. 293.
11. Francis A. Schaeffer, *The God Who Is There*, in *Francis A. Schaeffer
    Trilogy* (Crossway, 1990), p. 110.

12. L. T. Jeyachandran, 'Challenges from Eastern Religions', in Ravi Zacharias (ed.), *Beyond Opinion* (Thomas Nelson, 2007), p. 89.

13. Os Guinness, *Unspeakable: Facing Up to the Challenge of Evil* (HarperCollins 2005), p. 120.

14. Andrew Rippin and Jan Knappert (eds.), *Textual Sources for the Study of Islam* (University of Chicago Press, 1990), p. 129.

15. Gottfried Leibniz, *Theodicy: Essays on the Goodness of God, the Freedom of Man and the Origin of Evil* (1734).

16. Augustine, *Confessions*, Books IV–VIII.

17. Ravi K. Zacharias, *Can Man Live without God?* (Thomas Nelson, 1994), p. 182.

2. If God knew the world would be a place of suffering, then why did he create it?

1. Stephen Hawking, *The Grand Design* (Transworld, 2010), p. 117.

2. Stephen Hawking, *Black Holes and Baby Universes and Other Essays* (Bantam Books, 1993), p. 173.

3. Michael Ramsden, www.rzim.eu/how-can-i-believe-in-god-when-theres-so-much-suffering, RZIM *Pulse* magazine, June 2010.

4. Norman L. Geisler, *Baker Encyclopedia of Christian Apologetics* (Baker Academic, 1998), p. 173.

5. C. S. Lewis, *The Problem of Pain* (HarperCollins, 1940), p. 27.

6. Alfred Lord Tennyson, *In Memoriam A.H.H.* (1850), Canto 27.

3. If God is so powerful, then why doesn't he stop evil before it happens?

1. Voltaire, *Candide*, trans. Lowell Bair (Bantam, 1963[1759]), p. 16.

2. www.secondlife.com.

3. C. S. Lewis, *The Problem of Pain* (HarperCollins, 1940), p. 18.

4. Richard Dawkins, *The God Delusion* (Bantam Press, 2006), p. 23.

5. Stephen J. Wykstra, 'The Humean Obstacle to Evidential Arguments from Suffering: On Avoiding the Evils of "Appearance"', *International Journal for Philosophy of Religion* 16 (1984), pp. 73–93.

4. Surely religion is the cause of so much suffering?

1. Melanie Reid, *The Times* magazine, 27 August 2011, p. 11.

2. Richard Dawkins, *The God Delusion* (Bantam Press, 2006); this is a theme throughout the book.

3. Christopher Hitchens, *God Is Not Great: How Religion Poisons Everything* (Allen & Unwin, 2007), title page.

4. Keith Ward, *Is Religion Dangerous?* (Lion Hudson, 2006), pp. 8–10.

5. Dawkins, *God Delusion*, p. 191.

6. Alister McGrath, *Dawkins' God: Genes, Memes and the Meaning of Life* (Blackwell Publishing, 2005). pp. 91–96.

7. Ibid., pp. 50–51: 'I cannot know for certain but I think God is very improbable, and I live my life on the assumption that he is not there.'

8. Paul Vitz, *Psychology as Religion: The Cult of Self-Worship* (Eerdmans, 1977), p. 9; quoted in John Stott, *The Cross of Christ* (IVP, 2006), p. 268.

9. http://www.independent.co.uk/news/colombias-owngoal-star-shot-dead-1418013.html (accessed 16 March 2012).

10. This section was inspired by Keith Ward, *Is Religion Dangerous?* (2006), pp. 179–180.

11. http://www.world-nuclear.org/info/chernobyl/health_impacts.html (accessed 6 May 2012).

12. http://www.poemhunter.com/poem/hymn-of-man.

13. Alister McGrath, *The Twilight of Atheism* (Random House, 2004), p. 184.

14. Also see Exodus 20:13; Deuteronomy 5:17.

15. Also see Luke 6:27–31.

16. Also see Matthew 6; Mark 7; Luke 12 – 13.

17. Alister McGrath and Joanna McGrath, *The Dawkins Delusion* (SPCK, 2007), p. 47.

18. Amy Orr-Ewing, *But Is It Real?* (IVP, 2008); ch. 6 discusses hypocrisy in more detail.

19. Keith Ward, *Is Religion Dangerous?* (Lion Hudson, 2006), pp. 183–184.

20. Jackie Pullinger, *Chasing the Dragon* (Hodder & Stoughton, 2001).

21. http://www.justice.gov.za/trc/media/pr/1995/p951130a.html (accessed 19 March 2012).

22. http://news.bbc.co.uk/hi/english/static/northern_ireland/ understanding/events/eniskillen_bomb.stm.

23. Matthew Parris, 'As an Atheist, I Truly Believe Africa Needs God', 27 December 2008 http://www.thetimes.co.uk/tto/opinion/ columnists/matthewparris/.

5. If God exists, then does he care about my suffering?

1. See Amy Orr-Ewing, *Why Trust the Bible?* (IVP, 2005) and Lee Strobel, *The Case for Christ* (Zondervan, 2000) for more information.

2. John Stott, *The Cross of Christ* (IVP, 2006), p. 31.

3. Cicero, *In Defense of Rabirius*, in *The Speeches of Cicero*, trans. H. G. Hodge (Heinemann, 1927), p. 467; quoted in Stott, *Cross of Christ*, p. 30.

4. This section draws heavily from Stott, *Cross of Christ*, pp. 30–31.

5. Also see Isaiah 40:1; 61:1; Matthew 5.

6. *The Long Silence*, quoted in Stott, *Cross of Christ*, pp. 327–328.

6. Am I responsible for anyone else's suffering?

1. C. S. Lewis, The Screwtape Letters (HarperCollins, 2002), p. ix.

2. Michael Ramsden, *Beyond Belief* (Thomas Nelson, 2007), ch. 7, 'Conversational Apologetics', p. 144.

3. Clint Hill, *Mrs Kennedy and Me: An Intimate Memoir* (Gallery Books, 2012).

4. Richard Dawkins, *The God Delusion* (Bantam, 2006), p. 253.

5. Tim Keller, *The Reason for God* (Hodder & Stoughton, 2008), p. 192.

6. Robert Crampton, 'Yes, I Cried at the Nativity Too', *The Times*, 15 December 2009.

7. Why does God allow natural disasters and diseases?

1. Richard Dawkins, *River Out of Eden* (Phoenix, 1995), p. 133.

2. Annie Besant, *Why I Do Not Believe in God* (Freethought Publishing, 1887); quoted in Alister McGrath, *The Twilight of Atheism* (Doubleday, 2004), p. 183.

3. http://www.secularhumanism.org/index.php?section=main&page =manifesto.

4. John Lennox, *God's Undertaker: Has Science Buried God?* (Lion Hudson, 2007), pp. 47–57.

5. Alfred Wegener, *The Origin of Continents and Oceans* (1912).

6. Peter D. Ward and Donald Brownlee, *Rare Earth: Why Complex Life Is Uncommon in the Universe* (Copernicus Books, 2000), pp. 202–204.

7. Ibid., pp. 191–220.

8. R. S. Saunders, A. J. Spear and E. M. De Jong et al., 'Magellan Mission Summary', *Journal of Geophysical Research Planets* 97:E8 (1992), pp. 13,067–13,090.

9. J. E. Guest et al., 'Small Volcanic Edifices and Volcanism in the Plains of Venus', *Journal of Geophysical Research* 97:E10 (1992), pp. 15,949–15,966.

10. See http://www.solarviews.com/eng/venvolc.htm (accessed 19 March 2012).

11. http://www.britannica.com/EBchecked/topic/243638/ Great-Red-Spot.

12. Paul Davies, *God and the New Physics* (J. M. Dent & Sons, 1983), ch. 13, 'Black Holes and Cosmic Chaos'.

13. William Lane Craig, *On Guard: Defending Your Faith with Reason and Precision* (David C. Cook, 2010), ch. 5, 'Why Is the Universe Fine-Tuned for Life?'.

14. Alister McGrath, *A Fine-Tuned Universe: The Quest for God in Science and Theology* (Westminster John Knox Press, 2009).

15. Hugh Ross, *The Creator and the Cosmos* (NavPress, 1995), p. 117.

16. *National Geographic* http://greenliving.nationalgeographic.com/ leading-causes-global-warming-2177.html (accessed 22 March 2012).

17. *National Geographic* http://news.nationalgeographic.com/ news/2010/01/100121-hurricanes-global-warming/ (accessed 22 March 2012).

8. Can a broken story be fixed?

1. http://www.cnn.com/video/data/2.0/video/bestoftv/2010/08/ 05/ac.hitchens.on.cancer.god.cnn.html (accessed 19 March 2012).

2. C. S. Lewis, *The Last Battle* (HarperCollins, 1956), p. 221.
3. Quoted in Tom Wright, *Surprised by Hope* (SPCK, 2007), p. 16.
4. Ravi Zacharias, *Jesus among Other Gods* (Word, 2000), p. 122.
5. N. T. Wright, *The Resurrection of the Son of God* (Fortress Press, 2003), p. 127.

9. How do I move forward from here?

1. The Richard Dawkins Foundation for Reason and Science UK commissioned Ipsos MORI to carry out the research in the week immediately following the 2011 UK Census.
2. http://www.telegraph.co.uk/news/uknews/1504443/I-forgive-you-mother-tells-racist-thugs-who-killed-son.html (accessed 19 March 2012).
3. Tim Keller, *The Reason for God* (Hodder & Stoughton, 2009), p. 189.
4. http://uk-england.alpha.org/alpha/find-a-course.
5. www.christianityexplored.org/course/find.